THE OPENING TO
THE QURAN

بِسْمِ ٱللَّهِ ٱلرَّحْمَٰنِ ٱلرَّحِيمِ

قَدْ جَآءَكُم مِّنَ ٱللَّهِ نُورٌ وَكِتَٰبٌ مُّبِينٌ
يَهْدِى بِهِ ٱللَّهُ مَنِ ٱتَّبَعَ رِضْوَٰنَهُۥ سُبُلَ ٱلسَّلَٰمِ
وَيُخْرِجُهُم مِّنَ ٱلظُّلُمَٰتِ إِلَى ٱلنُّورِ بِإِذْنِهِۦ
وَيَهْدِيهِمْ إِلَىٰ صِرَٰطٍ مُّسْتَقِيمٍ

Truly there has come to you from God a light and a clear book with which God guides whoever follows His pleasure to the paths of peace. And He brings them out from the darkness into the light by His permission. And He guides them to the straight way.

— The Quran, 5:15–16

THE QURAN: INTERPRETATION IN CONTEXT

THE OPENING TO THE QURAN

Commentary & Vocabulary Reference of al-Fâtiḥa

AHMAD ZAKI HAMMAD

FOREWORD BY PROFESSOR
MUHAMMAD QUTB

Printed in the United States of America

Published by: *Quranic Literacy Institute (QLI)*
P.O. Box 1467 • Bridgeview, Illinois 60455

Cover design by A. Whiteman. Cover photography by A. Sanders. Both under commission of the Quranic Literacy Institute.

FRONT COVER PHOTOGRAPH: The door of the Kaʿba, the first House of God on earth, the foundations of which were raised by Prophet Abraham عليه السلام and his son, Ishmael عليه السلام. Today it lies at the center of the surrounding Sacred Mosque in Makkah. The only door of the Ancient House, it is overlaid with gold and is inscribed with verses of the Muslim scripture, the Quran.

ISBN (cloth): 0-9650746-0-9

The Opening to the Quran is printed on premium acid-free paper that is in compliance with standards set for alkaline papers by the American National Standards Institute, Inc. The paper's permanence is estimated at more than 300 years. The binding materials were chosen for strength, durability, longevity, and ecological concerns. The text is set in Palatino Diacritic, a special type to facilitate Arabic transliteration and the use of features special to Islamic literature, such as " ﷺ " and " عليه السلام ".

FOR

All in the English-speaking world who
may derive from this work, even in the
smallest degree, the impulse to seek divine
guidance for a meaningful life,
here and in the Hereafter

AND FOR

The very special people
who have immeasurably enriched my life
— as a son, a brother, a husband, a father,
a friend, a student, and a teacher —
and who have enabled me to enjoy an
ever-rewarding study of the Gracious
Quran and the graced Prophet ﷺ

TRANSLITERATION NOTE

The transliteration of Arabic names and terms into English follows a well-established scheme shown below.

Also, nearly every mention of the Prophet Muḥammad's ﷺ name is followed by the Arabic " ﷺ " which may be translated as "God bless him and give him peace," a prayer of endearment reflecting Muslim veneration for the Prophet ﷺ. Likewise, out of veneration " عليه السلام " appears after the names of other prophets mentioned (as well as Angel Gabriel عليه السلام), and it means "peace be upon him."

ء	’	ض	ḍ
ا	â *or* a	ط	ṭ
ب	b	ظ	ẓ
ت	t	ع	ᶜ
ث	th	غ	gh
ج	j	ف	f
ح	ḥ	ق	q
خ	kh	ك	k
د	d	ل	l
ذ	dh	م	m
ر	r	ن	n
ز	z	ه	h
س	s	و	û *or* u w (consonant)
ش	sh	ى	î *or* i *or* iyy y (consonant)
ص	ṣ		

QURANIC CITATION NOTE

Nearly each of the more than 300 references to the Quran's verses is cited following an established numerical system. For example, the third verse of the Quran's first sura is cited as *1:3* (the sura number followed by the number of the verse, separated by a colon).

CONTENTS

FOREWORD

In the Shade of the Quran by Muhammad Qutb *xi*

INTRODUCTION

The Starting Point: The Opening to the Book of Allah 1

1 INTERPRETATION

Arabic Text and English Interpretation 4

2 OVERVIEW

The Opening to the Universe of the Quran 6

The Meaning of al-Fâtiḥa in Brief 6

Al-Fâtiḥa in the Chronology of Revelation 8

3 COMMENTARY

A Light to the Straight Way 10

Names, Themes, and Meaning of al-Fâtiḥa 10

I. Beginning and Continuity (Verse 1) 12

II. Praise and Thankfulness (Verse 2) 13

III. Twin Mercies (Verse 3) 16

IV. The Day of Judgment (Verse 4) 16

V. The Moral Contract (Verse 5) 18

VI. The Way of the Worshipper (Verse 6) 23

VII. The Secrets of Grace (Verse 7) 24

Summary 28

4 RULES AND FACTS

Highlights Regarding al-Fâtiḥa 29

Reciting al-Fâtiḥa in Prayer *(Ṣalât)* 29

Saying "*Âmîn*" After Reciting al-Fâtiḥa 30

The Excellence of al-Fâtiḥa *30*
Invoking Allah's Help by Reciting al-Fâtiḥa *31*

5 VOCABULARY REFERENCE
The Revealed Word: The Terms of the Opening *33*
1. Bism[illâh]: *In the name [of Allah]* *35*
2. Allah: *[In the name of] Allah* *36*
3. Al-Raḥmân al-Raḥîm: *The All-Merciful, the Mercy-Giving* *39*
4. Al-Ḥamd: *All praise* *41*
5. Rabb: *Lord [of the Worlds]* *43*
6. ʿÂlamîn: *Worlds* *44*
7. Mâlik: *Master* *45*
8. Yawm: *Day* *48*
9. Dîn: *Judgment* *49*
10. Naʿbud: *We worship* *51*
11. Nastaʿîn: *We ask for help* *53*
12. Ihdinâ: *Guide us* *55*
13. Ṣirâṭ: *Way* *57*
14. Mustaqîm: *Straight [way]* *58*
15. Niʿma [Anʿamta]: *Grace* *62*
16. Maghḍûb: *Wrath* *64*
17. Ḍâllîn: *Those astray* *65*

6 NOTES *71*

7 BIBLIOGRAPHY *77*

8 ḤADÎTH INDEX *89*

9 QURANIC VERSE INDEX *97*

10 SUBJECT INDEX *103*

ACKNOWLEDGMENTS *113*

FOREWORD

In the Shade of the Quran

by

Prof. Muhammad Qutb

I HAVE LIVED with the Quran for a long time and through several lives. I lived with it once with the child's imagination, following its stories, picturing its various settings, envisioning myself standing like an eyewitness watching its events and characters in motion before me—not merely living with it but captivated by it.

One of the stories that affected me most was that of Moses عليه السلام with its detailed scenes of Pharaoh, the court magicians, and especially Moses speaking to his Lord, saying, *"My Lord, show me [Yourself], so that I may look upon You." [Allah] said, "You cannot see Me, but look upon the mountain. If it remains firm in its place, then you shall see Me. And when his Lord manifested Himself to the mountain, He made it crumble, and Moses fell down stunned"* (7:143).

I knew then, from my reading of the sura, that the mountain did not remain standing and Moses did not see his Lord. Yet each time I recited the sura, I anticipated, with a child's wonder, that perhaps this time the mountain would stay firm in its place and Moses would see his Lord! But always I would see the mountain quake and Moses fall down stunned. My sensibilities would undulate and the intensity of my emotions would swell as if I were reciting the verse for the first time.

I lived with the Quran another life with the ardor of a budding youth pursuing aspirations upon delicate wings soaring into orbs of light, eventually coming back down to earth, his heart alight with slivers of this bright world that nourished him until the next ascent. Something in the Quran drew me into it. Perhaps it was its inimitable style of expression and the spirituality of revelation, or the towering heights evinced in the behavior of the prophets, blessings and peace be upon them, their purity and depth of faith and endurance, the fervor with which they turned to Allah in ease and hardship, and their devotion to Him. Or was it Allah's pleasure with them and His aid to them that hovered about them like unfailing light?

Such feelings are difficult for a young person to define and harder still for one to sort out their sources from the motifs, the style, and the élan of the Quran. Yet at this stage one apprehends that the Quran harmonizes with his or her spirit, and one's spirit harmonizes with the Quran.

I lived with the Quran as a young man searching for the values and designs that govern the universe, life, humanity, and the ultimate ends of creation—not in pursuit of philosophy or because of a preoccupation with it, but in search of answers to the questions that compel a person who has become newly self-conscious: How and why did this entire existence come into being? Where did man come from? How should human life be on earth? Does one's life end when his or her limited time on earth expires? Why do small insects, barely visible, exist? Why do ferocious animals exist, which even when caged frighten human beings? Why do humans differ in such obvious ways, in looks, emotions, aptitudes, behaviors, and motivations? How are human beings to discipline their volatile urges and manage numerous ideas flying in every direction? How do they govern the diverse affairs and conflicting pressures of life? Such questions press upon human nature and demand answers.

I was then in the prime of my youth, and in my university years, when I used to read—and read much—in works of literature, science, and philosophy, all of which attempted to satisfy human nature's craving for answers, which proved trivial and incomplete. As for the fulfilling answer, it is found here, in the Quran.

I lived another life with the Quran searching for authentic methodologies applicable to literature, art, education, politics, economics, ethics, and so forth. From my university studies, I grew aware of some of these ideologies as they were practiced in Western societies. Based on life in the contemporary Middle Eastern society of which I was a part, I was also aware of its discordant intermixture of invading Western ideas and fading remnants of principles that were at some point rooted in Islam. I realized there were serious defects here and breaches there. I attempted to define them and discover their causes and consequences as far as my experience allowed and to the extent of my awareness of what was around me. At the same time, I was seeking a method free from imperfection in addressing these spheres of life. Yet in the end, I arrived at something that astonished me at the time: The much-pursued approach to all these domains was to be found in the Quran. In light of this discovery, I wrote four books on method: *Methodology of Islamic Art* (*Manhaj al-Fann al-Islâmî*); *Methodology of Islamic Education* (*Manhaj al-Tarbiya al-Islamiyya*); *Studies in Human Psychology* (*Dirasât fî Nafs al-Insâniyya*); and, concerning Islamic historiography, *On the Islamic Interpretation of History* (*Ḥawla al-Tafsîr al-Islâmî li al-Târîkh*).

I lived with the Quran, finally, in search of an inclusive system that covers every facet of life and at the same time furnishes the thread that interweaves all these aspects together, thereby yielding a universal answer that provides an orderly, consonant meaning to life, without rigidity or pretension. I sought this out especially in opposition to the ideology of communism, with its dialectic materialism and materialistic interpretation of history, which at that time appealed to a good many people but to me was untenable.

After long study, I found (and without surprise this time) this system in the Quran—the religion of life, which Allah Himself revealed so that humanity could dwell in justice. Thus He established in this Book the clear-cut foundation for all of man's needs, so that human life could be built on the evident foundation of righteousness on earth. He fixed within it humankind's way of worship, thought, and conduct, and the laws by which people are to govern their affairs, the horizons toward which they should aim their aspirations, and the values to which they are to adhere—if their human essence is indeed to be realized.

Again, after long study I found that this universal way is the real meaning of *Lâ ilâha illa'Allâh*, the witness that "There is no God but Allah," as the Quran illustrates it. Thus *Lâ ilâha illa'Allâh* is not simply the words pronounced by the tongue, nor is it merely the sentiment associated with them. It is the verbal substance and its emotional significance blended into a complete, comprehensive way of life that comprises all realms of human existence. These are some of the focal points of my long companionship with the Quran.

From time to time, I used to look into various English translations of the meanings of the Quran and would become greatly disappointed. How far they were from the original! How distant was the sense of atmosphere that ripples over one's spirit, thoughts, and emotions with the Quran when compared to the dry, forced atmosphere that these translations impart!

I myself did translation work at one stage of my life and understand its difficulties. I know with certainty that it is impossible to transmit from one language to another the entirety of a text of a literary work that carries not only intellective meaning but implications resulting from selecting specific words and arranging them in a particular, appropriate context. Hence poetry is even more difficult to translate than prose; in fact, to translate a poem into poetry in another language is a virtually impossible feat if one hopes to convey the identical feeling and range of meaning of the poem in the new host language.

If all of this applies to human speech, what of the Word of Allah, in which *inimitability* is an inherent quality, such that it defies the genius of masters of oration and eloquence to match it? Indeed, the translation of the Quran into an equivalent text in another language is a human impossibility. Yet, while knowing this, I nonetheless became greatly disappointed when reading some of the translations that came to me. The fact is that the Quran itself cannot be "translated" into any language in a way that approximates the Arabic in which it was revealed. But we can certainly translate the "meanings" of the Quran in a manner superior to the existing translations of many who have endeavored to contribute efforts in this field.

Many times I have asked myself: How should this much-needed translation be? What approach should be used? Should it be a literal translation? Should it be an explanation or interpretation that clarifies the intended meaning? Or perhaps it should be a word-for-word translation supported by an interpretation and explication that helps the reader to live in the environment of the Text.

Then my thoughts turned to another issue. Who would be best suited for such a translation? This person would have to be someone who had attained to an exact knowledge of the language of the Quran, as well as a precise awareness of the manner of speech of the language into which it will be translated.

Specifically, he should be one whose native tongue is Arabic, who could discriminate the nuances of the Arabic text by virtue of it being the language in which he reads, writes, speaks, thinks, and conveys himself, and who would therefore be able to comprehend the connotations of the Arabic text in addition to the meanings of its idioms. Thus he would be equipped to at least deliver a reasonable semblance of the affect and atmosphere of the Text, helping the reader of the target language to recover a meaning close to what is meant.

Years passed, and I found no one coming forward to face this monumental task (translating the meaning of the Glorious Quran) who had the requisite, precise familiarity with Arabic, together with deep and sound knowledge of the language into which he would translate. Then I came to know of Dr. Ahmad Zaki Hammad's initiative to embark upon this arduous endeavor. I empathize with him in the effort he faces and have trust that he is an Arab who possesses originality in the Arabic language, both by way of formal studies and by being seasoned in public discourse. In addition, as someone trained in the study of the *Sharîʿa*, he is more capable of comprehending the meanings of the Quran than those who have not had the opportunity to focus on Islamic disciplines, for though they may taste the beauty of the Quran, they are liable to miss much of its inferences.

Knowing that Dr. Ahmad Zaki Hammad possesses these qualities, that he is likewise fluent and proficient in the English language—reading, writing, and speaking it—and that there is a team of Muslims around him who are well versed in the English language and filled with zeal to serve Islam and the Book of Allah, I nonetheless have sympathy for him, and for them, concerning this effort, for I know how monumental this labor is, and how exhausting and difficult it can be. However, after reading the interpretation which is now before the reader, I felt assured that we were at last about to see a worthy translation of the meanings of the Glorious Quran in English, one that enables English speakers to live in the shade of the Quran and derive from it the guidance that their Lord wills them to acquire.

Sûrat al-Fâtiḥa in particular, despite its few verses and the economy of its words, conveys a great many deep, enlightening, distinct meanings, as though it were a concise summary of the topics and aims that the Quran treats. This is why the commentaries that the interpreter has written, in addition to translating the Text itself, are necessary components of translating the meanings of the Quran.

In the end, one may ask, Why all this effort? Is it necessary? Undoubtedly, yes! Muslims who do not speak Arabic, and therefore do not independently comprehend the meanings of the Quran, but who nevertheless strive to worship Allah through the recitation of His Book, hold the right to have the meanings of the Book of Allah introduced to them and have a legitimate need for these meanings to be explained and elucidated. Only then can they know in a more defined way what their Lord requires of them, what is the true nature of the religion they adhere to, and what is the true meaning of *Lâ ilâha illa'Allâh*—the declaration which they utter in the morning and the evening, whether expressed with their tongues or treasured in the depths of their souls.

As for non-Muslims, they too have a right upon us, namely, that we make clear to them the most accurate picture of Islam possible. They generally do not know Islam, except through distorted depictions—whether or not deliberately presented to them this way—or they know nothing of it at all. Their due claim on us is that we present them with the truth of Islam, so that when they consider it and make a determination, they will have been well informed about what they are reflecting on and the choices they make.

Indeed, this endeavor provides a genuine opportunity to carry through the chief mission of the Prophet ﷺ to which so much of his life-model pertains, namely, introducing the Quran to people who are unaware and clarifying it for them. I earnestly commend those who have undertaken this monumental work, and I pray for their success and ask Allah to benefit Islam, Muslims, and humanity by it.

And the last of our prayers is *All praise is for Allah, Lord of the Worlds*.

Makkah

INTRODUCTION

The Starting Point: The Opening to the Book of Allah

THE JOURNEY INTO the Quran starts with al-Fâtiḥa. Just as branches and fruits grow from a seed, the suras (or chapters) of the Quran and their verses come one after the other, introducing and elaborating the major themes and issues al-Fâtiḥa raises.

This book begins with an "Interpretation" that expresses the meaning of al-Fâtiḥa's Seven Oft-Repeated Verses in a way that keeps close to the original Text, but at the same time takes into account Arabic and English idioms (applying the method articulated in our study *The Quran: Interpretation in Context*). This has made it necessary to survey the major works in commentary literature (*tafsîr*) and to consult the main Arabic lexicons and linguistic references of a general nature, as well as those specializing in the Quran. This, God willing, shall remain our approach with the rest of the Quran.

Next comes the "Overview," a brief explanation of al-Fâtiḥa's verses for those desiring a concise statement of their immediate meanings. It also summarizes the sura's background, the circumstances and chronology of its revelation, and the impact it had on the Prophet ﷺ.

An extended "Commentary" follows, amplifying al-Fâtiḥa's verses, in terms of their collective message in the overall context of the Quran and their inspirational potency. The "Commentary" proceeds from the notion that familiarity with the essential message of the Book furthers one's comprehension of its words, verses, and suras; for, in our view, the Quran and its parts are mutually illuminating. (It serves commentator and reader alike to give this point due consideration when seeking out an explanation or understanding of the scripture of Islam.) Certainly, the opening sura of the Quran provides a context for the "Commentary" to present something of the essential message of the Book. Since the Quran transcends the worldly barriers of language, religion, culture, experience, color, gender, and so forth, the "Commentary" speaks to the timeless issues facing the human family. In particular, it addresses every reader of English open to guidance from the Lord of the Worlds.

Following the "Commentary" are "Rules and Facts" related to al-Fâtiḥa in terms of its application in worship, occasions for recitation, and other relevant matters.

The work concludes with the "Vocabulary Reference," devoted to explicating the key words of al-Fâtiḥa. It examines the Arabic and Quranic usages of each term, with references to facilitate access to the sources. As the interpretation of the whole Quran continues, the "Vocabulary Reference," God willing, should evolve into an independent companion dictionary of Quranic terms.

The observations and critiques received from readers of

preliminary drafts have confirmed the immense advantage gained by the varied backgrounds and experiences of our many reviewers. The need for comments from the general public and specialists continues, so that the ongoing work of *The Quran: Interpretation in Context* may attain a standard befitting its subject, the Quran, and its audience, the readers.

1

INTERPRETATION

Arabic Text and English Interpretation

(١) سُورَةُ الفَاتِحَةِ

مَكِّيَّةٌ وَآيَاتُهَا سَبْعٌ

بِسْمِ ٱللَّهِ ٱلرَّحْمَٰنِ ٱلرَّحِيمِ ﴿١﴾

ٱلْحَمْدُ لِلَّهِ رَبِّ ٱلْعَٰلَمِينَ ﴿٢﴾ ٱلرَّحْمَٰنِ ٱلرَّحِيمِ ﴿٣﴾

مَٰلِكِ يَوْمِ ٱلدِّينِ ﴿٤﴾ إِيَّاكَ نَعْبُدُ وَإِيَّاكَ

نَسْتَعِينُ ﴿٥﴾ ٱهْدِنَا ٱلصِّرَٰطَ ٱلْمُسْتَقِيمَ ﴿٦﴾

صِرَٰطَ ٱلَّذِينَ أَنْعَمْتَ عَلَيْهِمْ غَيْرِ ٱلْمَغْضُوبِ

عَلَيْهِمْ وَلَا ٱلضَّآلِّينَ ﴿٧﴾

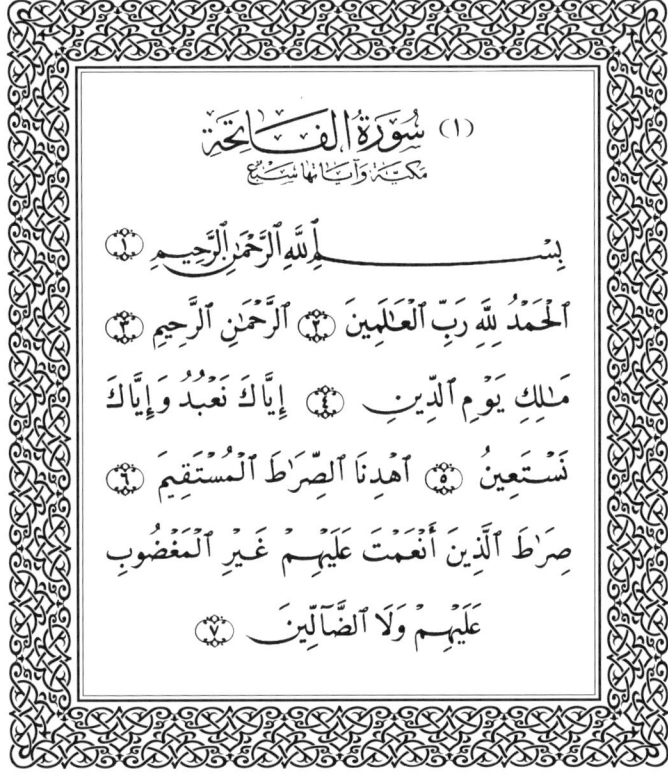

SURA ONE

AL-FÂTIḤA

THE OPENING

Revealed in Makkah. Seven verses.

1 In the name of Allah,
the All-Merciful, the Mercy-Giving.

2 All praise is for Allah,
Lord of the Worlds,

3 the All-Merciful, the Mercy-Giving,

4 Master of the Day of Judgment.

5 It is You we worship,
and it is You we ask for help.

6 Guide us to the straight way,

7 the way of those upon whom
You have bestowed grace,
not those upon whom there is wrath,
nor those astray.

2

OVERVIEW

The Opening to the Universe of the Quran

The Meaning of al-Fâtiḥa in Brief

AL-FATIḤA BEGINS ***in the name of Allah*** and with two attributes of His benevolence. He is ***the All-Merciful, the Mercy-Giving,*** extending His blessings to one and all. He is the Creator who nurtures His creation and sustains it, encompassing the furthest reaches of every being.

All praise is for Allah. He is the ***Lord of the Worlds,*** who knows all affairs, hears all pleas, responds to all needs. He is ***Master of the Day of Judgment***—the ruler of perfect justice, before whom all people, all beings, all issues shall come. Those who succeed will reside in perpetual delight, and those who fail will dwell in painful regret. But for those who say sincerely to their Lord, "***It is You we worship, and it is You we ask for help,***" a sacred trust is made between the needful human being and God, the Enricher, whose unfailing help provides strength, fulfills every rightful need, and safeguards one from vulnerabilities.

In quest of moral excellence, the fellowship of believers makes a collective appeal to God for lasting guidance upon His path: ***Guide us to the straight way***, the waymarks of which are not mere material gains or worldly achievements, but rather people blessed with spiritual wellness and moral ascendance, namely, ***those upon whom You have bestowed grace***.

The faithful, as much as they are able, remain true to both the letter and the spirit of God's commandments and so are saved from incurring His anger or straying into dogmatic error. They are, in other words, ***not those upon whom there is wrath, nor those astray***.

In essence, al-Fâtiḥa is a personal prayer centering the human spirit on the will of God as expressed in His final Revelation.* With its every recitation, the worshipper enters into intimate dialogue with God, as Prophet Muḥammad ﷺ related:

> Allah, the Almighty and the Majestic, has said, "I have apportioned the Prayer (al-Fâtiḥa) between Myself and My worshipper in two parts—and My worshipper shall have what he has asked for."
>
> So when the worshipper says, "*All Praise is for Allah, Lord of the Worlds*," Allah says, "My worshipper has praised Me."
>
> When he says, "*The All-Merciful, the Mercy-Giving*," Allah says, "My worshipper has extolled Me."
>
> When he says, "*Master of the Day of Judgment*," Allah says,

* For an elaborate treatment of the supplications of the Quran and the Prophet ﷺ, see my work, *Lasting Prayers of the Quran and the Prophet Muḥammad* ﷺ (Oak Lawn, IL: Quranic Literacy Institute, 1996).

"My worshipper has magnified Me and entrusted Me with his affairs."

When he says, "*It is You we worship, and it is You we ask for help,*" Allah says, "This is between Myself and My worshipper—and My worshipper shall have what he has asked for."

When he says, "*Guide us to the straight way, the way of those upon whom You have bestowed grace, not those upon whom there is wrath, nor those astray,*" Allah says, "This is for My worshipper—and My worshipper shall have what he has asked for."[1]

Al-Fâtiḥa is a beacon drawing one to the way of God, warning humanity to avoid wandering down every dark defile made to appear otherwise. To this the believers voice a resonant *Âmîn*: "O God, accept our prayer!"[2]

Al-Fâtiḥa in the Chronology of Revelation

The majority of Quranic authorities hold that al-Fâtiḥa was revealed shortly after the Prophet's first encounter with the Angel of Revelation in the Cave of Ḥirâ', near the top of the Mount of Light on the outskirts of Makkah; that is, following, in order of revelation, the opening verses of Sûrat al-ʿAlaq (96), then Sûrat al-Qalam (68), Sûrat al-Muddaththir (74), and Sûrat al-Muzzammil (73).[3]

The early Quranic verses sent down before al-Fâtiḥa addressed the Prophet ﷺ directly, preparing him for his new role and mission. They instructed him to believe in himself (68:2–4), to arise from seclusion and go forth to warn humankind of its fate, even in the glare of relentless public scrutiny (74:2–7), and to pray at length during the night (73:2–4). Understandably, he was at first worried and unsure. "When I am all alone, I hear a call, and, by God, I fear for myself!" the Prophet ﷺ confided in his wife Khadijah.[4] She suggested that he consult her learned cousin, Waraqa ibn Nawfal, a Makkan scriptural sage, who advised the Prophet not to turn away from the call, nor to fear it.[5]

The revelation of al-Fâtiḥa assured the Prophet, eased his mind, and detailed the early Quranic commands, particularly the first one: *Read in the name of your Lord who created* (96:1). With al-Fâtiḥa, he began experiencing a distinctive dimension of Islam: Direct, immediate communication from the worshipper to God, the self-subsisting source of all creation. It is here that the Prophet, peace be upon him, is first given voice in the context of revelation. In al-Fâtiḥa, the Quranic style shifts from instructing and addressing the Prophet, as in the earlier verses he received, to guiding him (and thereby the community of believers) to freely appeal to God Himself for aid and direction, and to do so with intensity and presence of mind and heart.

Classical and modern commentators, such as Zamakhsharî (d. 538/1143) and Muḥammad ʿAbdu (d. 1323/1905), who argue that al-Fâtiḥa is the first Quranic revelation, neglect the above context.[6] Others, like Mujâhid al-Makkî (d. 104/722), who hold that it was revealed after the migration to Madinah some thirteen years later, perhaps misread the Prophet's statement describing al-Fâtiḥa, together with the closing verses of Sûrat al-Baqara (2:285–86), as the "two lights [of revelation] without equal in the Torah, the Psalms, or the Gospel," since the latter verses from Sûrat al-Baqara were, in fact, revealed in Madinah.[7]

3

COMMENTARY

A Light to the Straight Way

Names, Themes, and Meaning of al-Fâtiḥa

"THE GREATEST CHAPTER of the Quran" is how the Prophet of Islam ﷺ described al-Fâtiḥa, which literally means "the Opening." The many other names it has come to acquire (exceeding thirty) show its preeminence in Muslim scripture, thought, and life. In recognition of its importance, it is called the "Mother," "Foundation," and "Essence" of the Quran. In terms of its relieving effect, it is said to be the chapter of "Healing" and "Sufficing." In measure of its value, it is the "Treasure." In form and function, it is the "Seven Oft-Repeated [Verses]" or, simply, the "Prayer," since it is the center of Muslim ritual Prayer (*Ṣalât*)* and is recited at least seventeen times daily during the five obligatory Prayers.[8]

Al-Fâtiḥa, however, is more widely known as the chapter of "Praise," Sûrat al-Ḥamd, after the proclamation be-

* "Ritual Prayer" refers to the precise manner of performing *Ṣalât* prescribed by God and demonstrated by the Prophet ﷺ.

ginning its second verse, *All praise is for Allah*, for it teaches the mortal how to express praise and thankfulness to God for the gift of life and what sustains it and makes it meaningful.*

The sura summarizes the major themes of Islam. At its center is the sole Creator and one's purity of faith and reverence for Him. Al-Fâtiḥa awakens the senses to the numerousness of His creation and the vital, active realm in which humankind lives, urging the mind to contemplate its perfect Maker and the profound need for His mercy and guidance. Al-Fâtiḥa reveals that human nature recognizes God and that each soul aspires to be close to Him, a hope fulfilled so long as one earnestly seeks refuge in Him from fruitless knowledge, wicked motives and ends, and the hazards of ignorance and confusion.

The verses of al-Fâtiḥa uplift the heart from a vague, passive feeling about God to a knowing, willing worship of Him. They inspire one to persistently seek His help and mercy to freely enjoy the upright life. The mind al-Fâtiḥa shapes detests swerving from the godly path; the spirit it fashions avoids incurring His displeasure or drifting among those who have strayed.

Al-Fâtiḥa is a guiding star in the expansive universe of the Quran. It affirms the covenant with the Lord of All People. It states the believer's mission; it reminds one to consider deeply the state of his or her soul; and it reawakens a person to his or her relationship with the rest of humanity—the righteous, the wrongdoing, and the indifferent—and with all things in this worshipping universe. Thus, al-

*See *Al-Ḥamd* in the "Vocabulary Reference," pp. 41–43.

Fâtiḥa is more than an ordinary prayer in the movement of good against evil. It is a promise to uphold the higher truths and to honor the earlier proponents and communities of righteousness, seeking, in a way, their company, by learning from their triumphs and tribulations in this life and aspiring to their real success in the Hereafter. Simply, al-Fâtiḥa's thirty-one words state the essence of being human, in reliance and dependence on the Creator.

I. Beginning and Continuity بِسْمِ اللَّهِ الرَّحْمَٰنِ الرَّحِيمِ

Al-Fâtiḥa is the moral center of the Quran, opening *in the name of Allah, the All-Merciful, the Mercy-Giving*, the source of creation, life, and guidance. There is no God but Him, the Knower of the unseen and the seen. He is the Peace and the Faithful, the Guardian and the Overpowering, the Irresistible and the Proud, the Creator and the Sustainer, the First and the Last, the Manifest and the Hidden, who neither begets nor is begotten, and *to whom belong the most excellent names* (20:8).

The first words of the Quran revealed to the Prophet instructed him to *read in the name* of his Lord (96:1), and al-Fâtiḥa's opening verse fulfilled this commandment, initiating a fundamental Muslim ethic: To invoke the name of God in carrying out the affairs and concerns of everyday life. The reason is clear and simple: To direct human activity in God's name and for His pleasure, preserving the integrity of one's motives and actions from foul inclinations and corruption.

The formula, *In the name of Allah, the All-Merciful, the Mercy-Giving* (known as the *basmala*), perfected for the

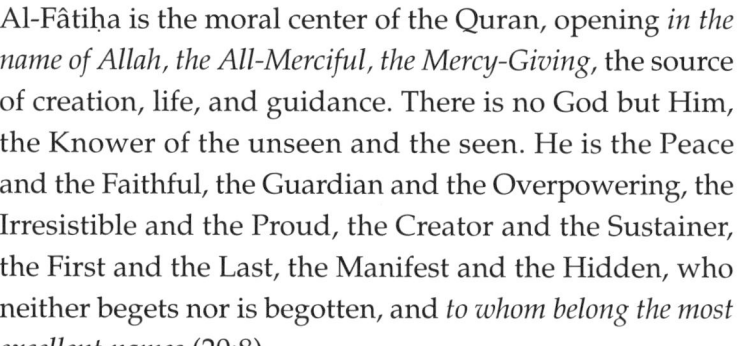

Prophet ﷺ and for all humanity the etiquette of righteous beginnings. It saves human sensibilities from being misdirected by subjective assertions or random commencements and cultivates a sense of spiritual purpose; for invoking the name of God awakens one's heart to His remembrance, a distinguishing feature of the Islamic character. One arises and sleeps, eats and drinks, enters and exits, speaks and listens, explores and learns, makes contracts and transactions, marries and enjoys marital relations *in the name of Allah,* conscious that each act relates to His worship.

To begin an act in the name of the One who originated existence and endowed it with beauty and utility is to take a stand for belief in the true and only God and to reinforce a continuity with preceding believing men and women, stretching back to Adam and Eve, the parents of humanity. Beginning otherwise is to be disconnected from the source and heritage of faith. The Prophet ﷺ said, "Any significant act that does not begin 'in the name of Allah' is severed," that is, cut off from reward or benefit.[9]

II. Praise and Thankfulness ٱلْحَمْدُ لِلَّهِ رَبِّ ٱلْعَٰلَمِينَ

Mentioning the name of God in fear and in hope liberates a person from self-centeredness and despair. The human soul finds peace and fulfillment in this remembrance, and the relationship between the worshipper and his or her Lord is renewed. One recalls, as the well-known tenth century Quran commentator al-Ṭabarî stated, "the incalculable bounties He has bestowed upon His servants," and that He has "endowed [their] organs with health so that He can be obeyed, and strengthened the limbs of the body so that His commands can be performed."[10] Free and inspired, the human being acquires a tenacity of purpose for advancing the conditions of life, raising its moral standards, and shepherding its resources to fruitful and ethical ends.

The Muslim heart not only beats with reverence for God, but it also becomes naturally thankful for life's treasures of sustenance, shelter, relationships, well-being, knowledge, dignity, and other favors of God. The worshipper is moved to express praise for Him and His hallowed attributes and to glorify His splendor. The phrase commencing al-Fâtiḥa's second verse, *All Praise is for Allah,* becomes the anthem of Muslim life and its moral imperative. Every major theme of worship—as enunciated in al-Fâtiḥa—resides in the very essence of giving praise and showing gratitude. Ibn ʿAbbâs, a Companion of the Prophet renowned for his knowledge of the Quran, said:

> *Al-ḥamdulillâh* (All praise is for Allah) is the word of every thankful person. . . . Noah said, *"All praise is for Allah who has delivered us from the wrongdoing people"* (23:28). And Abraham said, *"All praise is for Allah who has granted me, despite old age, Ishmael and Isaac"* (14:39). And David and Solomon said, *"All praise is for Allah who has favored us over many of His believing servants"* (27:15). And Allah said to His Prophet (Muḥammad), *"Say, All praise is for Allah who has not taken a son"* (17:111). And the residents of the Garden will say, *"All praise is for Allah who has removed grief from us"* (35:34)—and the last of their prayers is, *"All praise is for Allah, Lord of the Worlds"* (10:10). It is truly the word of every thankful person.[11]

By cultivating a grateful relationship with the Creator, the believer also becomes disposed to show due gratitude to creation. This is the seed of respect for other forms of existence that inspires one to help preserve the delicate balances within nature. Moreover, one is impelled to acknowledge the good deeds, benevolent works, and charity of others. "Whoever does not thank people does not thank Allah," the Prophet ﷺ said, revealing the wider connection of relations among human beings as based on their relationship with God.[12] Indeed, the life of the Prophet ﷺ is literally a model of gratitude. As the first recipient of the Quran, he set the pattern for responding to God with thankfulness and praise, as in this prayer, which the Prophet ﷺ often said during the night:

> O Allah, for You is all praise! You are the light of the heavens and the earth. For You is all praise! You are the Sustainer of the heavens and the earth. For You is all praise! You are the Lord of the heavens and the earth and all therein. You are the Truth. Your promise is the truth. Your word is the truth. The meeting with You is true. The Garden is true. The Fire is true. The Hour is true.
>
> O Allah, to You I submit. In You I believe. On You I rely. To You I repent. For You I oppose. To You I refer in judgment. So forgive me whatever I may have done and whatever I may do, whatever I have concealed and whatever I have revealed. You are my God. There is no God but You.[13]

The Muslim temperament reserves such sublime praise and gratitude for God alone. Celebrating His praises brings one into harmony with everything else in the worshipping universe. *Whatever is in the heavens and whatever is in the earth give glory to Allah. To Him belongs the kingdom and to Him belongs all praise. And He has power over all things* (64:1).

How can it be otherwise when He is the Lord of the atoms and the galaxies, of people and beasts, of the seen and the unseen? Moreover, His Lordship is free from the limitations of space, time, and any other variable and dimension. Nor is it exclusive to a branch of the human family or any past or future generation. He sustains the whole of creation and extends an encompassing benevolence to each of its creatures in every condition. He hears all prayers and is responsive to every need. All are cherished by the *Lord of the Worlds*.

III. Twin Mercies ٱلرَّحْمَٰنِ ٱلرَّحِيمِ

After proclaiming God's praise and unrivaled sovereignty over the universe, al-Fâtiḥa's third verse, *the All-Merciful, the Mercy-Giving*, restates these twin attributes of His kindness and clemency, for He showers His mercy upon both the responsive and the unresponsive among His creation. It stresses the full, pervasive touch of His mercy, which extends to every being that is, has been, or will be. Nothing is beyond its reach.

A person's hope expands with the realization that the endless shade of God's mercy overspreads everything in existence. The Prophet ﷺ said, "Allah has a hundred mercies. It is through one of these mercies that all creatures show mercy to one another, while ninety-nine mercies remain [with Him] for the Day of Resurrection."[14]

IV. The Day of Judgment مَٰلِكِ يَوْمِ ٱلدِّينِ

Beginning *in the name of Allah*, raising His praise, acknowledging His dominion, and professing His mercy, al-Fâtiḥa then reveals something more about Allah: He is *Master of the Day of Judgment*. At the end of earthly time,

He will hold each soul accountable for its performance in life. This allusion to the final reckoning imparts to the individual, in a flash of insight, the entire flow of human existence—life, death, resurrection, and then felicity or misery. Such crucial ends, hinging on this unique event of human destiny, raise the urgent questions of mortal life: Who am I? Where did I come from? Where am I going? What road shall I travel? What is good and what is evil? What is the way to ultimate success?

This heightened consciousness prepares the worshipper for the moral contract introduced in the next verse. Yet here al-Fâtiḥa discloses God's unshared sovereignty over the Day of Judgment. Nearly every subsequent chapter of the Quran states, elaborates, or reinforces the reality that existence extends beyond the confines of this world and that believing in the afterlife attests to faith in God.

The verse, *Master of the Day of Judgment*, recalls the purpose of life as the Creator intended it and reminds one of the final reckoning. In this sense, the fourth verse of al-Fâtiḥa is an answer to the mission of man and his soul-searching. It brings one to the realization that the same God who originated creation will certainly—indeed, easily—revive each individual from the dust of death. *By my Lord, you will certainly be raised, and then you will certainly be informed of what you have done. That, for Allah, is easy* (64:7).[15] The gift of life first breathed into the Children of Adam will be breathed into them again—not to relive this earthly life (sleeping, waking, working, searching, competing, winning, and losing), but to enjoy God's reward for the good one has performed and to be accountable for doing otherwise. *Thus, whoever has done an atom's weight of good shall see it, and whoever has done an atom's weight of evil shall see it* (99:7–8).

Having certainty in a never-ending afterlife fulfills human nature's yearning for everlasting existence and ultimate justice. Secure in its promise, believing men and women are not lulled into apathy. On the contrary, they aspire—here and now—to liberate themselves from the constraints of temporal existence, including the ills of disease and disorder, the harms committed against one another, the oppression of superstition and ignorance, the tyranny of chauvinistic ideologies and authoritarian systems, and the limitations of the physical senses and the dimensional world. It is in part the realization of the spiritual and moral potential for advancement and excellence, or regression and depravity, that moves one to assume responsibility for one's self, one's family, and the state of affairs in the immediate society or in the global community.

V. The Moral Contract إِيَّاكَ نَعْبُدُ وَإِيَّاكَ نَسْتَعِينُ

Al-Fâtiḥa's mention of the *Day of Judgment* thus opens a window for the alert human conscience to glimpse the enduring consequences of even its slightest actions. At this juncture, the hope-filled worshipper calls out to the Lord of the Worlds for His ever-extended assistance: *It is You we worship, and it is You we ask for help.* We learn from the Prophet ﷺ that al-Fâtiḥa is God's answer to this cry of the heart. God states, said the Prophet ﷺ :

> O son of Adam, I have sent to you seven [verses]: Three for Me, three for you, and one between you and Myself.
>
> As for the three of Mine, they are: *In the name of Allah, the*

> *All-Merciful, the Mercy-Giving*; *All Praise is for Allah, Lord of the Worlds*; and *the All-Merciful, the Mercy-Giving*.
>
> As for the three for you, they are: *Master of the Day of Judgment*; *Guide us to the straight way*; and *the way of those upon whom You have bestowed grace, not those upon whom there is wrath, nor those astray*.
>
> The one between us is, *It is You we worship, and it is You we ask for help* (meaning *worship* from the worshipper and *help* from Allah, the Exalted).[16]

Implicit in the appeal, *It is You we worship, and it is You we ask for help*, is one's covenant with God. It is the ultimate agreement, the moral contract, as if one were to say, "Only You we adore, You we obey, Your guidance we accept, and Your commandments we desire to fulfill. Help us, then, to succeed in attaining true worship of You." The courage to voice, and thereby endorse, this contract is a full realization of what it means to be human. It is the birth of a fresh and enduring relationship between the created soul and the creating Lord. A person announces his or her devotion and intention to comply with God's will, and then asks the Help-Giver to increase His abundant blessings.

Worship then becomes the sanctuary of the whole of human existence, the criterion of righteousness and values, the motive of behavior. This shift in perspective regarding worship enables one to focus on the substantial and to dismiss the superfluous. This is captured in a well-known supplication of the Prophet ﷺ :

> O Allah, You are my Lord. There is no God but You. You created me, and I am Your servant. I uphold Your covenant and promise, as much as I am able. I seek refuge in You

> from the harm of whatever I may have done. To You I acknowledge Your grace upon me, and to You I bring my sins. Forgive me, for truly no one forgives sins except You.[17]

It is then for Allah to accept this initiative and bestow His love and mercy upon such cultivated humanness, granting to His worshippers what they ask. God has stated, according to the Prophet's narration:

> O My servants, all of you are astray but those whom I guide; so seek guidance of Me, and I shall guide you. O My servants, all of you are hungry but those I feed; so seek food of Me, and I shall feed you. O My servants, all of you are naked but those I clothe; so seek clothing of Me, and I shall clothe you. O My servants, you err by night and by day, and I forgive all sins; so seek forgiveness of Me, and I shall forgive you.[18]

Every human being who matures into sound adulthood makes a choice whether to be a worshipper of God or not. Those who elect to express and thus enter into the moral obligation alluded to in al-Fâtiḥa commit themselves to a way of life marked by precision and expanse. It is a moral contract touching every sphere, comprehending each act, and outlasting death. This way of life begins with the first flicker of conscious purpose in the human breast; for every breath and step, every thought and utterance, and every prayer and deed constitute worship if done with the intention to please God. When it comes to the scope of worship, nothing lies outside its realm. It is by nature indivisible and in motive unshared. What belongs to God is His, and whatever is rendered unto any other is likewise His.

Worship is both timeless and germane—original to all things that have been and that will be, appropriate to the existence of each varied worshipper, and relevant to every evolving condition. Moderate and accommodating, worship is responsive to the limitations of the ill, the minor, and those with disabilities, exempting them from all or part of its ritual requirements. Similarly, it opens limitless horizons for the human spirit to excel in goodness and surpass marginality.

But worship is not encumbering, for one aspect of it does not hinder another. After learning of three youthful Companions who had taken vows to pray all night without rest, fast every day without break, and remain celibate, the Prophet of Islam ﷺ said, "I pray in the night and I sleep; I fast and I break my fast; and I marry women."[19] Moderation, therefore, is inherent in worship. *Allah intends for you ease, and does not intend for you difficulty* (2:185).

Worship conserves the balance in relations, whether between a worshipper and God, one person and another, or humankind and the rest of creation, so that one calls out to the Originator, *Our Lord, give us good in this life and good in the Hereafter, and protect us from the torment of the Fire* (2:201). And it reminds people to *do good as Allah has been good to you* (28:77). Worship preserves one's spiritual purity, intellectual vision, and emotional equilibrium. Submission to the will of God—the All-Trustworthy, the Guardian, the All-Preserving—saves the human being from ruin and emptiness.

Yet, in the end, the choice to be made is to affirm or to reject bound service to God. Those who accept may advance to the highest station in life and are hopeful of eternal peace in the Hereafter, for they gain honor and ascendancy by serving their Lord in this world. This sense of stewardship is the much sought after link by which one sheds feelings of loneliness and alienation, and draws nearer to God. The model worshipper, Muḥammad, peace and blessings be upon him, often expressed his submission and servanthood to God, praying that the Quran would remain the indwelling guidance of his heart:

> O Allah, I am indeed Your servant, the son of Your servant, the son of Your maidservant. My forelock is in Your hand. Your decree upon me is done, and Your judgment upon me is just. I beseech You by every one of Your names—with which You have named Yourself, or have taught to any one among Your creation, or have sent down in Your Book, or have kept to Yourself in the knowledge of the unseen—to make the Quran the springtime of my heart, the light within my chest, the departure of my sadness, and the vanishing of my worries.[20]

Worship in Islam assumes commitment, especially in personally establishing the rites God has enjoined upon people, including Prayer (*Ṣalât*), Fasting (*Ṣiyâm*), Almsgiving (*Zakât*), and Pilgrimage (*Ḥajj*). Yet human beings may not always sustain the full extent of their performance, may violate promises and agreements—by intent or neglect—or even forget themselves amidst life's particularities. For this al-Fâtiḥa instructs people to seek strength and aid from the source of power and vitality: *It is You we ask for help*. The Prophet ﷺ exhorted his Companions to appeal for God's help after each Prayer: "O Allah, help me to remember You always and be thankful to You, and to worship You in the most excellent way."[21] Zamakhsharî notes that the petition for help in this verse is universal, encompassing everything one seeks God's help in achieving. He adds, "It is best to ask for His help and guidance in fulfilling the duties of worship with the verse, *Guide us to the straight way,* thus defining the help sought."[22]

VI. The Way of the Worshipper اهْدِنَا الصِّرَاطَ الْمُسْتَقِيمَ

After willingly entering into a moral covenant with the Master of the Day of Judgment, the worshipper voices the culminating prayer of al-Fâtiḥa, asking God to grant whatever may safeguard and facilitate this compact: *Guide us to the straight way.* Ibn Kathîr (d. 774/1372), a well-known Quran commentator, says of this verse, "In every hour and in every condition, a worshipper is in need of Allah, the Exalted, to keep him firm on the way of guidance, thoroughly familiar with it, clear-sighted in it, enriched by it, and continuing on its course."[23] He then cites a statement of the Prophet ﷺ that illustrates the significance of adhering to the straight way and overcoming the temptations along its path:

> Allah has given the likeness of a straight way. On both sides of this way are two walls with open doors. On the doors are hanging drapes. At the gateway is a caller who says, "O people, enter the way all together, and do not turn off from it," along with another caller calling from [deep] within the way. When a person desires to open any of these doors, the [latter] caller says, "Woe to you! Do not open it, for if you open it, you will enter it." The way is Islam. The walls are the limits Allah has set. The open doors are the prohibitions of Allah. The caller at the head of the way is the Book of Allah. The caller within the gateway is the warner of Allah in the heart of every Muslim.[24]

The human quest for direction is indeed al-Fâtiḥa's major theme. Its reward is endless bliss among the righteous, a blessing conferred by the Eternal on the mortal. The simple petition, *Guide us to the straight way*, is filled with aspiration and hope, as if one were to implore:

> O God, show us its landmarks, its guidelines, its standards. Inspire us to seek out its signs and traces, to comprehend its truths and realities. Teach us to revere its guiding principles and to look toward its heavenly ends. The straight way is beloved by us, so make its norms dear to us. We have embarked upon it, so grant us the ability to continue our journey, and make our feet firm upon it. Help us overcome any obstacles in its path. Protect us against straying from the moderation and evenness of its way.

The worshipper reaches the peak of human goodness with this plea, seeking guidance not only for him- or herself but for all (*guide "us"*) who by the same moral contract have bound themselves to God's Way (*It is You "we" worship, and it is You "we" ask for help*). There is no greater charity.

VII. The Secrets of Grace

صِرَٰطَ ٱلَّذِينَ أَنۡعَمۡتَ عَلَيۡهِمۡ غَيۡرِ ٱلۡمَغۡضُوبِ عَلَيۡهِمۡ وَلَا ٱلضَّآلِّينَ

In al-Fâtiḥa, living by revealed guidance and its principles expresses adherence to "the straight way," a path identified by its adherents, *those upon whom You have bestowed grace*, and distinct from the way of *those upon whom there is wrath* and *those astray*. This single verse transcends worldly barriers and makes a definitive statement on the unchanging nature of true belief and faith in the one Creator, namely, closeness to God lies not in the circumstances of birth or life, but in the convictions of one's soul.

Knowing the characteristics of those upon whom God has bestowed grace is vital to the believer. The Quran details elsewhere what is briefly stated in al-Fâtiḥa. In Sûrat Maryam, for example, Noah, Abraham, Ishmael, Isaac, Jacob, Moses, Aaron, Zechariah, John, Mary (for whom the sura is named), and Jesus are identified as among the foremost of those *upon whom God has bestowed grace, among the prophets of the Children of Adam, and among those whom We carried with Noah, and among the children of Abraham and Israel, and among those whom We have guided and chosen* (19:58).

The Quran shows that these models of grace shared a common virtue and standard of belief: *When the signs of the All-Merciful were recited to them, they fell down in prostration, weeping* (19:58); that is, their distinctiveness lay in the disposition to be responsive to God and to accept and submit wholeheartedly to His will, without resistance. Out of reverence for Him and from the joy of their profound gratitude for the blessing of faith that had descended upon them, their tears flowed. To their ranks the Quran adds the *truthful*, the *martyrs*, and the *righteous* (4:69). This highlights another defining quality of those upon whom grace has been bestowed, namely, a willingness to sacrifice.

In reflection upon this verse—*the way of those upon whom You have bestowed grace, not those upon whom there is wrath, nor those astray*—the worshipper comes to a keen realization: Choice is a foundation of belief, and where there is choice, there are alternatives and the potential for opposition. This is a subtle but penetrating reminder that the straight way has a moral objective whose preservation and implementation may call for the sacrifice of that which is valued and loved, even life itself.

Just as it is vital for one treading the straight way to know the qualities of the people of grace, it is equally important to recognize the characteristics of the people of wrath and others who are astray, namely, those who willfully breach their covenant with God or attribute to Him what they have no knowledge of. The Prophet, peace be upon him, after his migration to Madinah, explained that the verse *those upon whom there is wrath* refers to the Children of Israel who deliberately and repeatedly violated their covenant with God and abandoned the laws of Moses, and that the words *those astray* make reference to Christians who have forsaken the teachings of Jesus and ascribed to God and His prophets what He did not authorize. This concluding appeal—not to be like *those upon whom there is wrath, nor those astray*—refers to any people who abandon, reject, or manipulate revealed truth.[25]

To accept and adhere to the upright way of life, believing in eternal salvation and reward, or to reject faith and stray along diverse paths is essentially left to each individual, since belief cannot be forced into anyone's heart. Thus, its native approach is effective presentation, gentle persuasion, and dialogue. The pattern of disbelief, however, is to silence, banish, or intimidate, that is, to suppress interaction. The Quran illustrates this by contrasting the uprightness and compassion of Abraham with the intolerance and ruthlessness of his *straying,** idol-worshipping father:

> *When [Abraham] said to his father: "My dear father, why do you worship what can neither hear, nor see, nor avail you in any-*

* "Straying" is the description the Quran records of Abraham's father in 26:86.

> *thing? My dear father, indeed knowledge has come to me that has not reached you. So follow me, and I shall guide you to an even way. My dear father, do not worship Satan, for surely Satan is rebellious to the All-Merciful. My dear father, I fear that a torment from the All-Merciful will strike you so that you will become a patron of Satan."*
>
> *[His father] said: "Are you averse to my gods, O Abraham? Surely, if you do not stop, I will stone you. So part from me for a long while."*
>
> *[Abraham] said: "Peace be upon you! I shall ask my Lord to forgive you. Indeed, He has been ever gracious to me. And I shall stay away from you and whatever you call upon apart from Allah."* (19:42–48)

Hence, it is foreign to the nature and the logic of Islam that one should be passive in belief and not share it with others, for it is the inalienable right of every person to hear the words of the Lord of creation and have access to His guidance, *so that those who perish might perish with clear proof, and that those who live might live with clear proof* (8:42). This is the trust which Muḥammad ﷺ left to each Muslim—male and female, in every era—in his Farewell Address: "Let whoever is present convey [the message] to whoever is absent, for [the latter] may comprehend better than one who first heard it."[26]

Indeed, with the blessing of guidance comes the sincere hope that Allah will foster this grace among one's peers and among future generations, and that all will be saved from going astray or displeasing their most merciful Lord. Uttering this prayer—to be guided on the straight way of the blessed—sets the worshipper upon the path of righteousness with a firm resolve to follow it *in the name of*

Allah, the All-Merciful, the Mercy-Giving. One is well served by the memory of Prophet Muḥammad ﷺ who, upon emerging from his dwelling and starting on his way, would turn his face toward the heavens and say:

> In the name of Allah, I rely on Allah. I seek refuge in You from straying or being led astray, from erring or slipping into error, from oppressing or being oppressed, from ignorance or from the ignorance of others against me.[27]

Summary

Of all the verses Allah has revealed, He chose al-Fâtiḥa to be repeated in each standing of every Prayer (*Ṣalât*). Whatever the ultimate wisdom may be, perhaps the significance of this resides in the human need to be constantly reminded of the essential truths of life and that which gives it direction. The truths that al-Fâtiḥa keeps in the forefront of one's mind are no less than the major themes of the Book it opens: Faith in the true and only merciful God; gratitude to the Sustainer of all being; certainty in the Day of Judgment; sincerity in worship and seeking God's help; a resolve to adhere to the straight way of the rightly guided of all ages; and avoidance of the ways of the rebellious, the trespassers, and the lost.

4

RULES AND FACTS

Highlights Regarding al-Fâtiḥa

Reciting al-Fâtiḥa in Prayer (Ṣalât)

IN RECOGNITION OF al-Fâtiḥa's importance in Islamic worship and Muslim life, the Prophet ﷺ said, "There is no Prayer for those who do not recite the Opening of the Book."[28] This has been interpreted by scholars in various ways. Some hold that it is necessary to read al-Fâtiḥa in the obligatory Prayers (*Ṣalât*), meaning that this fundamental rite of worship requires the inclusion of al-Fâtiḥa, such that ritual Prayer becomes invalid without it.[29] Others are of the opinion that Prayer performed without its recitation is imperfect.[30]

If one cannot recite al-Fâtiḥa—as in the case of a new or non-Arabic-speaking Muslim or someone with an impediment—a faithful recitation of its meaning in one's native language or to the extent of one's capacity may suffice until he or she is able to understand and recite the Arabic text properly. At that point, it becomes obligatory or, as others say, at least very desirable to do so. Other supplications may be substituted in the meantime, such as, "O Allah, shower me with Your mercy, save me from all harm, and maintain my well-being; guide me and provide for me."[31]

Saying "Âmîn" After Reciting al-Fâtiḥa

After completing the recitation of al-Fâtiḥa, it is preferable to say, "*Âmîn*," essentially meaning, "O Allah, answer my prayer."[32] Moreover, the Prophet ﷺ said to his Companions, "When the imam (the leader of the Prayer) says, *Not those upon whom there is wrath, nor those astray*, then say, '*Âmîn.*' Whoever's utterance [of '*Âmîn*'] coincides with that of the angels shall have their sins forgiven."[33] The Prophet ﷺ said "*Âmîn*" in an audible voice, as did those who prayed with him, in the vocalized portions of the Dawn, Sunset, and Evening Prayers.[34] Ḥanafî and Mâlikî scholars,* however, hold that saying "*Âmîn*" should always be silent, relying on various reports from Ibn Masᶜûd and other Companions.[35]

The Excellence of al-Fâtiḥa

"Once I was praying in the mosque," narrated Abû Saᶜîd ibn al-Muᶜalla, a Companion of the Prophet, "and the Prophet, peace be upon him, called me, but I did not respond to him [until finishing the Prayer]. 'O Messenger of God,' I later said, 'I was praying.'

"[The Prophet ﷺ] then said, 'Did Allah not say, "*Respond to Allah and to the Messenger when he calls you. . . .*"?' (8:24).

"Then he said to me, 'Shall I not teach you the greatest

*For an introduction to the major principles governing juristic variance, see my book, *Islamic Law: Understanding Juristic Differences* (Indianapolis: ATP, 1992).

sura of the Quran before you leave the mosque?' and he took my hand.

"So when we wanted to leave, I said, 'O Messenger of Allah, you said, "I shall teach you the greatest sura of the Quran." '

"[The Prophet ﷺ] said, '*All praise is for Allah, Lord of the Worlds.* It is the Seven Oft-Repeated [Verses] and the magnificent Quran that has been given to me.' "[36]

Invoking Allah's Help by Reciting al-Fâtiḥa

Al-Fâtiḥa was recited in the time of the Prophet, peace and blessings be upon him, to invoke God's help for the sick and injured. In one instance, according to Abû Saʿîd al-Khudry, some Companions of the Prophet were traveling when a young girl came running to them and said, "The chief of this area has been stung and our men are away. Are any of you healers?"

So one of the Companions, whom the others had never known to be associated with healing, went with her. He then recited something over the chief, who thereafter recovered and rewarded the Companion with thirty goats and milk to drink. When he returned, the others said to him, "Have you ever before healed in this manner?" "No," he said. "I only recited [over him] the Mother of the Book (al-Fâtiḥa)."[37] When they returned to the Prophet ﷺ and related the story to him, he approved of this action.

Also, during times of drought, the Prophet ﷺ recited verses from al-Fâtiḥa when asking God for rain.

All praise is for Allah, Lord of the Worlds, the All-Merciful, the Mercy-Giving, Master of the Day of Judgment. There is no God but Allah. He does what He wills. O Allah, You are the only God, there is no God but You, the Self-Sufficient. And truly we are in need, so bring down to us rainfall. And let what You have brought down for us be a [source of] strength and means for a time.[38]

5

VOCABULARY REFERENCE

The Revealed Word: The Terms of the Opening

THE WORDS OF al-Fâtiḥa (the Opening) make up the basic vocabulary of worship. Their steady flow, one into the next, gives the sura its matchless economy, impact, and spiritual temperament.

The first concepts the sura introduces relate to Allah—His mercy, praiseworthiness, lordship, sovereignty, and judgment. Ideas oriented toward the individual follow, namely, worship, help, guidance, the straight way, grace, wrath, and straying. Together these concepts express the sweep of Islam and the mission of its believing community. To comprehend the value of these Arabic words, to glimpse their history, and to gain a feel for their Quranic usage are important goals for every student of the Quran. The English renderings of the interpretation of al-Fâtiḥa have been selected with reverence for the Quran's universality. A presentation of the sura's key words—noting concrete and extended meanings, Quranic usages, and, occasionally, statements of the Prophet ﷺ — helps readers to reinforce their grasp of the English interpretation and to better their understanding of the original text.

The purpose of this chapter is not to assemble a mere Quranic word list as an index. Rather it provides readers with an account of the meanings, Quranic usages, and linguistic development and derivatives of the principal words of al-Fâtiḥa. Each word is entered according to the sequence in which it appears in the sura. The root letters are noted in Arabic script. The references and their page numbers following each entry facilitate further study and access to the sources. The italicized words in the right column correspond to the transliterated Arabic terms on the left.

1. Bism[illâh]	*In the name [of Allah]*
2. Allah	*[In the name] of Allah*
3. Al-Raḥmân al-Raḥîm	*The All-Merciful, the Mercy-Giving*
4. Al-Ḥamd	*All praise*
5. Rabb	*Lord [of the Worlds]*
6. ʿÂlamîn	*Worlds*
7. Mâlik	*Master*
8. Yawm	*Day*
9. Dîn	*Judgment*
10. Naʿbud	*We worship*
11. Nastaʿîn	*We ask for help*
12. Ihdinâ	*Guide us*
13. Ṣirâṭ	*Way*
14. Mustaqîm	*Straight [way]*
15. Niʿma [Anʿamta]	*Grace*
16. Maghḍûb	*Wrath*
17. Ḍâllîn	*Those astray*

1. Bism[illâh]: In the name [of Allah]

ISM (اسم): From the Arabic root, س م و. ***Ism*** (pl. *asmâ'*) is the name of a thing, a designation that may be uttered or written, acknowledging what is named. It may also distinguish the substance or an attribute of a thing, as in the Quran's description of a spring in Paradise "named" *Salsabîl* (76:18) or in reference to Allah teaching Adam "the names" (2:31), that is, enabling him to distinguish or identify things. From the same origin comes the word *samâ'* for "sky," "heaven," or what is elevated, that is, something raised to notice, making it known. Thus, *ism* also signifies "fame," "renown," and "repute." When *ism* is prefixed by the Arabic preposition *bi,* it means "in" or "with" the name, as in *bismillâh,* meaning "in the name of Allah."

Several other derivatives are applied in the Quran. From *samma* comes the "naming" of Mary by her mother (3:36); Abraham "designating" the believers as "the Muslims" (22:78); and disbelievers "assigning" female "names" to angels (53:27).

Asmâ', the plural of *ism,* is used in reference to Adam learning *the "names," all of them* (2:31), and to Joseph exposing idols and false deities as mere "names" without reality or authority (12:40).

With reference to Allah, *asmâ'* refers to His divine attributes, such as being the All-Merciful, the Everlasting, and the All-Forgiving. The Quran says that *His are the most excellent "names"* by which believers appeal to Him and invoke Him (20:8, 59:24). Stemming from the same root is *samiyya,* as in the verse affirming that Allah has no "equivalent" in eminence or glory (19:65).

The form *musammâ*, occurring twenty-one times (always accompanied by the word *ajal*, "period" or "term"), means "set," as in a period or term being stated, fixed, specified, or appointed. For example, the Quran says that the sun and moon run their courses for an "appointed term" (31:29, 35:13); Allah causes the developing fetus to remain in the womb for an "established term" until birth (22:5); people are aroused from sleep until their "determined period" of death (39:42); the believers are to record in writing loan agreements that are for a "fixed term" (2:282); and the heavens, earth, and all between them are created for a "specified term" (30:8, 46:3).

REFERENCES: ʿAbd al-Bâqî, *al-Muʿjam al-Mufahras*, pp. 361–66; Abû ʿÛda, *al-Taṭawwur al-Dalâlî*, pp. 249–50; al-Fayrûz-abâdî, *Baṣâ'ir Dhawî al-Tamyîz*, 3:262–66; Ibn al-Jawzî, *Nuzhat al-Aʿyun al-Nawâẓir*, 1:237–38; Ibn Manẓûr, *Lisân al-ʿArab*, 14:397–403; Lane, *Arabic-English Lexicon*, 4:1433–35; Majmaʿ al-Lughat al-ʿArabiyya, *Muʿjam Alfâẓ al-Qur'ân al-Karîm*, pp. 311–13; Mûsâ, *Qâmûs Qur'ânî*, pp. 31–32, 376; Muṣṭafâ, *al-Muʿjam al-Wasît*, pp. 452–53; al-Sayyid, *al-Afʿâl fî al-Qur'ân al-Karîm*, 2:723; al-Zabîdî, *Tâj al-ʿArûs*, 10:182–84; al-Zamakhsharî, *Asâs al-Balâgha*, pp. 220–21.

2. *Allah: [In the name of] Allah*

ALLAH (الله): From the Arabic root, ا ل ه. ***Allah***, the true and only God, is one of the most frequently occurring terms in the Quran, appearing 2,810 times, and the most recognized of Islamic names. Preceded by "*ism*" and prefixed by the Arabic preposition "*bi*" in the phrase *bismillâh*, the name "Allah" appears in al-Fâtiḥa's first verse in the well-known formula, *in the name of Allah*.

Arabic linguists—modern and classical—trace the

term's origin to the Arabic verb *aliha/ya'lahu*. Some, though, assert that it derives from Aramaic or Hebrew. The existence of similar words in other languages is not, however, conclusive in establishing linguistic precedence, meaning that one language did not necessarily borrow from another, especially since the languages and usages spoken of are fairly ancient. Indeed, the form and application of the word "Allah" suggest its genuine origin in the Arabic language. In pre-Islamic times the word *ilâh*, from *aliha/ya'lahu*, was used by the ancient Arabs to invoke a supernatural power or authority for protection and security.

The verb *aliha* denotes seeking refuge, protection, and aid for preservation; to save, rescue, or deliver from evil; or to render one safe and secure. It also means to remain or abide, as well as to confound or perplex the mind by the greatness or majesty of something (in this case, God). The addition of the definite article "*al*" (according to some linguists) forms the word "Allah."

It is noteworthy that the word *Allah* has no record of being used, even by pre-Islamic Arabs, for anything other than the Supreme Being. Al-Ghazâli states that the meaning of the name *Allah* is "so specific, it is inconceivable that it be shared, either metaphorically or literally." He further states:

> *[Allah]* is the name for the true existent, the one who unites the attributes of divinity, is subject of the attributes of lordship, and unique in true existence. For no existent thing other than He may claim to exist of itself, but rather it gains existence from Him. . . . For everything *is perishing except His Face* (28:88). It is most likely that in indicating this

meaning, [the word *Allah*] is analogous to proper names, so everything which has been said about its derivation and definition is arbitrary and artificial.[39]

The formula, *In the name of Allah, the All-Merciful, the Mercy-Giving* (known as the *basmala*), appears as an introduction to each sura, with the exception of the ninth, Sûrat al-Tawba.[40] It also occurs in Sûrat al-Naml (27:30). Moreover, it is the universal commencement of formal discourses and documents, the importance of which is poignantly stated by the Prophet ﷺ when he said, "Any significant act that does not begin 'in the name of Allah' is severed," meaning, cut off from reward or benefit.[41]

The expression "in the name of Allah" (*bismillâh*), without qualifying attributes, occurs only one time in the Quran, when Noah orders those accompanying him to embark on the Ark *in the name of Allah* (11:41). The phrase "name of Allah," however, appears in nine places, as in the instruction to eat that over which the *name of Allah* has been mentioned (6:118, 119) and glorifying the *name of Allah* during *Ḥajj* (Pilgrimage) or in places of worship (22:28, 40). The construction "in the name of your Lord" (*bismirabbik*) appears in the Quranic injunction to *glorify the "name" of your Lord* (69:52) and *remember the "name" of your Lord in the morning and evening* (76:25).

REFERENCES: ʿAbd al-Bâqî, *al-Muʿjam al-Mufahras*, pp. 38–75; Abû ʿÛda, *al-Taṭawwur al-Dalâlî*, pp. 89–95; al-Aṣfahânî, *al-Mufradât*, p. 17; al-Fayrûzabâdî, *Baṣâ'ir Dhawî al-Tamyîz*, 2:1230; Ibn Manẓûr, *Lisân al-ʿArab*, 13:467–71; Lane, *Arabic-English Lexicon*, 1:82–83; Majmaʿ al-Lughat al-ʿArabiyya, *Muʿjam Alfâẓ al-Qur'ân al-Karîm*, pp. 23–24; Muṣṭafâ, *al-Muʿjam al-Wasîṭ*, p. 25; al-Zabîdî, *Tâj al-ʿArûs*, 9:374–76; al-Ẓâhirî, Abû Turâb, *Shawâhid* *al-Qur'ân*, pp. 563–74; al-Zajjâjî, *Ishtiqâq Asmâ'illâh*, pp. 23–32; and al-Zamakhsharî, *Asâs al-Balâgha*, p. 9.

3. *Al-Raḥmân al-Raḥîm: The All-Merciful, the Mercy-Giving*

AL-RAḤMÂN (الرَّحمن) and ***AL-RAḤÎM*** (الرَّحيم): From the Arabic root, ر ح م . ***Al-Raḥmân*** and ***al-Raḥîm*** are derived from the word *raḥma*, meaning "mercy," implying tenderness, kindness, and benignity.

Al-Raḥmân and *al-Raḥîm* are two of Allah's *excellent names* (59:24) that express His endless mercy. From the same root comes *raḥim*, the place sustaining life before birth, that is, the "womb." It is considered the connecting element in relations among relatives, such as parents and children. The link between *raḥma* and *raḥim* reflects the highest degree of tenderness and compassion, as characterized by the nature of motherhood and the sharing of sustenance and care with the developing life before and after birth. In acknowledging the importance of kinship and the role of motherhood, the Prophet ﷺ said that in describing His designation of the womb as *raḥim*, Allah has stated, "I am *al-Raḥmân* (the All-Merciful) and have created the *raḥim* (the womb) and derived its name from Mine. So whoever brings it close, I will bring close [to Myself]; and whoever severs it, I will sever."[42]

The Quran uses several derivatives of the base word *raḥma*, as *marḥama*, "sympathy"; *arḥâm*, "relatives"; *râḥim*, "agent of mercy" or having mercy; and, in reference to Allah, *al-Raḥmân*, "the All-Merciful"; *al-Raḥîm*, "the Mercy-Giving" or "the Beneficent"; and *Dhû'l-Raḥma*, "Possessor of Mercy." In its most common usage, *raḥma* refers to the sustaining favor and love Allah bestows upon His creation, for His mercy encompasses everything (7:156).

In extended application, the Quran (7:52), as well as the Torah of Moses (11:17), is proclaimed to be *raḥma*, "a mercy," for it lights the way to Allah's mercy. Similarly, Allah proclaims Muḥammad ﷺ to be "a mercy to the worlds" (21:107) and Jesus "a mercy" (19:21). The Quran also characterizes the relationship among believers as one marked by *raḥma*, "mercy" (48:29).

While *al-Raḥmân* is an adjective describing Allah and is among His most often cited attributes (appearing fifty-seven times in the Quran), it is not merely descriptive but intensive as well, expressing perfection and fullness in mercy. So exclusive is *al-Raḥmân* in referring to Allah that it is the foremost synonym for His proper name, as in the verse, *Say, "Call upon Allah or call upon al-Raḥmân," whichever [name] you call upon, for His are the most excellent names* (17:110). *Al-Raḥmân* indicates having mercy forever and without limit. The English rendering of *al-Raḥmân* as "the All-Merciful" embraces both His unending mercy and its magnitude.

While *al-Raḥmân* signifies possessing the utmost degree of mercy, *al-Raḥîm* indicates the intensity and generosity of its application. Occurring ninety-five times in the Book, it is used primarily in contexts where divine mercy is imparted, connoting its movement from the source of mercy to its recipients as a force in this world—hence, the translation "the Mercy-Giving."

Elsewhere in the Quran, *raḥîm* is used more specifically in connection with believers: Allah bringing them out from darkness into light and ever extending His mercy to them (33:43) and their endearment to the Prophet ﷺ, moving him to accord them compassion and mercy (9:128). Thus, the term "mercy-giving" maintains the balance between richness in mercy and the lavish bestowal of mercy that the word *al-Raḥîm* describes. The alternative translations of "compassionate" and "benevolent" imply emotional sharing, while "beneficent" is frequently used without a sense of volition; also "benignity" emphasizes self-serenity. These words stress the disposition of one who is mercy-giving rather than suggest the actual dispensing of mercy. Finally, the interpretation "the All-Merciful (*al-Raḥmân*), the Mercy-Giving (*al-Raḥîm*)" is more reflective of the Arabic text, applying one base word—"mercy" for *raḥma*—to these twin attributes that share a common root and complement each other in meaning.

REFERENCES: ʿAbd al-Bâqî, *al-Muʿjam al-Mufahras*, pp. 304–9; Abû ʿÛda, *al-Taṭawwur al-Dalâlî*, pp. 107–10; al-Aṣfahânî, *al-Mufradât*, pp. 196–97; al-Fayrûzabâdî, *Baṣâ'ir Dhawî al-Tamyîz*, 3:53–58; Ibn al-ʿImâd, *Kashf al-Sarâ'ir*, pp. 73–76; Ibn al-Jawzî, *Nuzhat al-Aʿyun al-Nawâẓir*, 1:215–18; Ibn Manẓûr, *Lisân al-ʿArab*, 12:232–33; Lane, *Arabic-English Lexicon*, 3:1055–57; Majmaʿ al-Lughat al-ʿArabiyya, *Muʿjam Alfâẓ al-Qur'ân al-Karîm*, pp. 242–44; Mûsâ, *Qâmûs Qur'ânî*, pp. 184–89, 190; Muṣṭafâ, *al-Muʿjam al-Wasîṭ*, p. 335; al-Sayyid, *al-Afʿâl fî al-Qur'ân al-Karîm*, 2:560–61; al-Zabîdî, *Tâj al-ʿArûs*, 8:305–8; al-Zamakhsharî, *Asâs al-Balâgha*, p. 158.

4. *Al-Ḥamd: All praise*

ḤAMD (حَمْد): From the Arabic root, ح م د . ***Ḥamd*** is praise, exaltation, glorification, or commendation for a helpful action or favor, connoting approval or satisfaction. It further signifies the recompensing or rendering of due rights for a course of action or as a consequence of conduct.

The root of *ḥamd* occurs in the Quran sixty-eight times in various forms, most often in relation to praising Allah, from whom all blessings come. He is praised for being the Lord of the Worlds (1:2, 45:36); for creating the heavens and the earth (6:1); for making darkness and light (35:1); for being just to wrongdoers (6:45); for giving guidance (7:43); for revealing the Quran to the Prophet (18:1); for being the sole God who neither begets nor has partners (17:111); for providing relief and safety (23:28, 35:34); and for granting victory (110:3).

The Quran reveals that Allah is praised at all times by all things in the heavens and earth (17:44). Natural phenomena, such as thunder, extol Him, as do supernatural beings, namely, angels and jinn; for He is praiseworthy in every circumstance and condition (2:267). Although praising Allah is obligatory, according to the Quran, a person's conscious praise of Him is volitional, making it an explicit act of belief (9:112), while its neglect is an act of arrogance and disbelief. The only occurrence of *ḥamd*, or "praise," in the Quran that does not relate to Allah is a stern warning to people not to be like those who pursue and enjoy receiving unmerited praise (3:188).

Other derivatives of *ḥamd* in the Quran include the name "Muḥammad," literally meaning one who is frequently praised, occurring four times (3:144, 33:40, 47:2, 48:29). A single reference is made to "Aḥmad," one of the Prophet's bestowed names, describing one who has reached a state recognized as deserving praise or commendation (61:6). Another derivative of *ḥamd* is found in the reference made to a promised *Maqâm Maḥmûd*, "Station of Praise," reserved for the Prophet, peace and blessings be upon him, in the Hereafter (17:79).

REFERENCES: ʿAbd al-Bâqî, *al-Muʿjam al-Mufahras*, pp. 217–18; Abû ʿÛda, *al-Taṭawwur al-Dalâlî*, pp. 305–9; al-Aṣfahânî, *al-Mufradât*, p. 130; al-Fayrûzabâdî, *Baṣâ'ir Dhawî al-Tamyîz*, 2:499–500; Ibn al-Jawzî, *Nuzhat al-Aʿyun al-Nawâẓir*, 1:146–47; Ibn Manẓûr, *Lisân al-ʿArab*, 3:155–58; Lane, *Arabic-English Lexicon*, 2:638–40; Majmaʿ al-Lughat al-ʿArabiyya, *Muʿjam Alfâẓ al-Qur'ân al-Karîm*, pp. 155–56; Muṣṭafâ, *al-Muʿjam al-Wasîṭ*, p. 196; al-Sayyid, *al-Afʿâl fî al-Qur'ân al-Karîm*, 1:386; al-Zabîdî, *Tâj al-ʿArûs*, 2:339–41; al-Zamakhsharî, *Asâs al-Balâgha*, p. 94.

5. Rabb: Lord [of the Worlds]

RABB (رب): From the Arabic root, ر ب ب. ***Rabb*** is a comprehensive term meaning "Lord" (or lowercase "lord"), owner, sovereign, one to whom obedience is due, such as a guardian, governor, or one in authority or command; or one who rears, fosters, or nourishes, as a caretaker who gradually helps nurture something or someone to a state of completion, maturity, or independence. Hence, the word *rabîb* (pl. *rabâ'ib*) means one "reared" or "raised," specifically, a child raised by his or her stepfather. *Rabb* is likewise applied to one who accomplishes or completes a task. Another signification is the act of collecting, as in the gathering of rain clouds, or putting affairs into an established, proper order.

Rabb is the second most frequently used reference for God, after "Allah," occurring 979 times in the Quran. It is often used in connection with the realms of Allah's Lordship, as in *Lord of the heavens and the earth* (17:102), *Lord of the Throne* (9:129), *Lord of the east and west* (26:28), *Your Lord, Lord of your forefathers* (26:26), or *Lord of the Worlds* (*ʿÂlamîn*), the latter occurring thirty-six times, including in al-Fâtiḥa (1:2). In various Quranic contexts, *rabb* indicates an owner, master, authority, or someone who bestows favors (12:41, 42, 50); some of its derivatives carry shades of this meaning. The term *ribbi* (pl. *ribbiyyûn*), for instance, denotes a well-versed scholar or master of religious knowledge (3:146), while *rabbânî* occurs in reference to people among the Israelites endowed with this knowledge (5:44, 63). The plural *arbâb* is used only in a condemnatory sense when compared with the term's primary signification, as when Joseph rhetorically asks his prisonmates, *Are various "lords" better, or Allah, the One, the All-Dominating?* (12:39).

REFERENCES: ʿAbd al-Bâqî, *al-Muʿjam al-Mufahras*, pp. 285–99; Abû ʿÛda, *al-Taṭawwur al-Dalâlî*, pp. 121–27; al-Aṣfahânî, *al-Mufradât*, pp. 189–90; al-Fayrûzabâdî, *Baṣâ'ir Dhawî al-Tamyîz*, 3:29–30; Ibn Manẓûr, *Lisân al-ʿArab*, 1:399–409; Lane, *Arabic-English Lexicon*, 3:1002–7; Majmaʿ al-Lughat al-ʿArabiyya, *Muʿjam Alfâẓ al-Qur'ân al-Karîm*, pp. 233–36; Mûsâ, *Qâmûs Qur'ânî*, pp. 279, 291, 443–44; Muṣṭafâ, *al-Muʿjam al-Wasîṭ*, p. 321; al-Zabîdî, *Tâj al-ʿArûs*, 1:260–65; al-Zamakhsharî, *Asâs al-Balâgha*, p. 150.

6. ʿÂlamîn: Worlds

ʿÂLAMÎN (عالمين): From the Arabic root, ع ل م. **ʿÂlamîn** (sing. *ʿâlam*) comes from the word *ʿalm*, which indicates the influence, visible impression, or effect of something (such as a mark, trace, color, finish, or decoration); something raised in an open place to serve as a guide or a milestone; a mark or sign by which something or someone is known; or a symptom. In general, *ʿalama* connotes the functions, effects, or indications of things that exist.

In concrete usage, *ʿâlam* means "seal" or that by which something is marked; that is, it is considered an authenticating device that indicates or proves the existence of its originator. In the Quran, *ᶜâlam* is a synonym for "creation," connoting every kind of created thing in the universe, including the earth, all its inhabitants, and everything on it. *ᶜÂlam* strongly denotes the "worlds" of rational beings, specifically humans, jinn, and angels. *Rabb al-ᶜâlamîn*, then, is the Lord of all beings, all things—large or small, seen or unseen, material or spiritual, animate or inanimate—all systems, planes, and dimensions; in short, the "Lord of the Worlds." The term "worlds" comes closest to carrying the sweeping inclusiveness that *ᶜâlamîn* connotes, while maintaining its plural signification.

The word *ᶜilm*, or knowledge, shares the same root as *ᶜâlamîn*. This is a logical derivative, since *ᶜâlamîn* refers to all that is knowable, of which only Allah has perfect knowledge, while intelligent beings, namely, humans, angels, and jinn, have varying degrees of awareness.

REFERENCES: ᶜAbd al-Bâqî, *al-Muᶜjam al-Mufahras*, pp. 469–81; al-Aṣfahânî, *al-Mufradât*, pp. 355–57; al-Balkhî, *al-Ashbâh wa al-Naẓâ'ir*, pp. 217–18; al-Fayrûzabâdî, *Baṣâ'ir Dhawî al-Tamyîz*, 4:88–95; Ibn al-ᶜImâd, *Kashf al-Sarâ'ir*, pp. 287–88; Ibn al-Jawzî, *Nuzhat al-Aᶜyun al-Nawâẓir*, 2:56–57, 2:61–63; Ibn Manẓûr, *Lisân al-ᶜArab*, 12:416–22; Lane, *Arabic-English Lexicon*, 5:2138–41; Majmaᶜ al-Lughat al-ᶜArabiyya, *Muᶜjam Alfâẓ al-Qur'ân al-Karîm*, pp. 432–36; Mûsâ, *Qâmûs Qur'ânî*, p. 190; Muṣṭafâ, *al-Muᶜjam al-Wasîṭ*, p. 624; al-Sayyid, *al-Afᶜâl fî al-Qur'ân al-Karîm*, 2:945–54; al-Zabîdî, *Tâj al-ᶜArûs*, 8:405–8; al-Zamakhsharî, *Asâs al-Balâgha*, p. 312.

7. Mâlik: Master

MÂLIK (مَالِك): From the Arabic root, م ل ك . ***Mâlik*** is derived from the word *mulk* (also *milk* or *malk*). The verb *malaka* means to acquire, take into possession, own, or lay hold of; to dominate; to exercise power, control, or authority over; to overwhelm; to have the status of mastership, rulership, or legitimate sovereignty over someone or something; or to wed.

Appearing 128 times in the Quran, the most striking usages of *mulk* and its derivatives refer to Allah's absolute sovereignty and ownership of all creation in its every form and component. The Quran speaks of the heavens and earth, and all between them, as being under Allah's dominion (2:107, 3:189), including aspects such as life and death or sight and hearing (10:31). Indeed, Allah's ownership is comprehensive, for He is *Mâlik al-Mulk,* Master of All Domains, meaning Owner of all possessions, Ruler of all realms, earthly and heavenly, Sovereign of all sovereignty (3:26). He is also sole Master of the treasure houses of mercy (17:100) and sustenance (16:73).

Just as Allah grants and restricts provision from His limitless stores according to His wisdom, He also withdraws and gives of His authority (*mulk*) to and from whomever He chooses (3:26). Acknowledging this, Solomon prayed for an earthly kingdom and dominion unattainable by anyone after him (38:35), and Joseph considered being entrusted with *something of the kingdom* as a favor of Allah upon him (12:101). Moreover, no one is allowed to intercede for others without Allah's permission (19:87, 43:86). Thus, entities—real or invented, physical or incorporeal, good or evil—called upon instead of Allah cannot exert any power over even a single atom in the heavens or earth (34:22). They are not capable of bringing or effecting any benefit or harm to anyone or anything. Nor can they thwart Allah's blessings or punishment (5:76).

Indeed, Allah's *blessedness* is announced by the very fact that He holds in His hand all dominion without any partner in authority (25:2, 67:1). And on Judgment Day, Allah will manifest before creation His sovereignty as it is, sublime and perfect (6:73, 25:26). On that day, no one will be able to benefit or harm another (34:42).

The mastership denoted in *Mâlik Yawm al-Dîn* (Master of the Day of Judgment) is a perfect and absolute ownership that is perpetual, unconditional, and exclusive. None besides Allah is entitled to dominion over the Day of Judgment, since He is the sole owner of creation and its destiny and everything associated with it, including knowledge of the Hour signaling the end of temporal existence. In this sense, *mâlik* indicates not only possession or authority, but the capacity to control, handle, or dispose.

In other contexts, *malik* refers to a title of a person who rules over others, as when the Israelites urged their Prophet to appoint a "king" over them (2:246–47); when the "king" of Egypt disclosed his dream, asking people in his court to seek its interpretation (12:43); or when the Queen of Sheba warned against the destructive potential of invading "kings" (27:34). Also, the idiomatic expression *mâ malakat aymânuhum*, "what their right hands possess," occurs several times in the Quran (in the second person plural and singular, as well), referring to what a person owns or has legitimate control or guardianship over; in Arabic what lawfully belongs to a person is figuratively referred to as being in the possession of one's right hand. Finally, among the delights of the Garden in the Hereafter is beholding "a great kingdom," *mulkan kabîra* (76:20).

The root of the term *malak* (pl. *malâ'ika*), "angel," which occurs eighty-eight times in the Quran, is related to the root of *mâlik*, but is listed under a separate entry.

REFERENCES: ʿAbd al-Bâqî, *al-Muʿjam al-Mufahras*, pp. 673–76; al-Aṣfahânî, *al-Mufradât*, pp. 492–94; al-Fayrûzabâdî, *Baṣâ'ir Dhawî al-Tamyîz*, 4:520–24; Ibn Manẓûr, *Lisân al-ʿArab*, 10:491–97; Lane, *Arabic-English Lexicon*, 8:3023; Majmaʿ al-Lughat al-ʿArabiyya, *Muʿjam Alfâẓ al-Qur'ân al-Karîm*, pp. 629–31; Mûsâ, *Qâmûs Qur'ânî*, pp. 224, 384, 425; Muṣṭafâ, *al-Muʿjam al-Wasîṭ*, p. 886; al-Sayyid, *al-Afʿâl fî al-Qur'ân al-Karîm*, 3:1297–98; al-Zabîdî, *Tâj al-ʿArûs*, 7:180–85; al-Zamakhsharî, *Asâs al-Balâgha*, p. 436.

8. *Yawm: Day*

YAWM (يوم): From the Arabic root, ي و م. ***Yawm*** (pl. *ayyâm*) literally means "day," the period between the rising of the sun and its setting, or dawn to dusk. It also refers to any day of the week, such as Thursday or Friday; an unspecified time, past or present; or an age marked by the prominence of a person or thing, such as the pre-Islamic era known as the "Days of Ignorance." When it alludes to a specific event, *yawm* may refer to a conflict or contention, as, for example, the "Day of Badr," referring to the Battle of Badr, in which the emerging Muslim community first engaged and defeated the disbelievers of Quraysh. *Yawm* also alludes to devastating events (41:16, 54:19).

Yawm as used in al-Fâtiḥa is clearly eschatological, since it pertains to the event of events at the end of time, when all people will be brought for ultimate judgment before God and recompensed individually.

Although *yawm* appears in the Quran 475 times, it most commonly signifies the end of temporal existence and entry into the Hereafter, usually modified by an adjoining term that describes that day or its events, as in *the Last Day*

(2:8, 62); *the Resurrection Day* (2:85); *the Day of No Doubt* (3:9, 25); *the Great Day* (10:15); *the All-Embracing Day* (11:84); *the Day All are Raised* (15:36); *the Known Day* (15:38); *the Day of Regret* (19:39); *the Day of Sorting* (37:21); *the Day of Reckoning* (38:16, 26, 53); *the Day of Calling* (40:32); *the Day of Eternity* (50:34); *the Day of the Emerging* (50:42); *the Day of Assembly* (64:9); *the Day of Mutual Disillusionment* (64:9); *the Promised Day* (85:2); and *the Day Secrets are Revealed* (86:9).

In other usages, *yawm* retains its temporal signification, but as a unit of time to help people relate to the origin of creation. For instance, Allah says that He created the heavens and the earth in six "days" (32:4), although "days" with Allah are immensely greater in duration than days measured according to earthly time. For example, reference is made to the Day of Reckoning as equaling fifty-thousand years (70:4), with another reference to a single day of Allah's as equaling one thousand years (22:47, 32:5).

REFERENCES: ʿAbd al-Bâqî, *al-Muʿjam al-Mufahras*, pp. 775–82; al-Aṣfahânî, *al-Mufradât*, p. 578; al-Balkhî, *al-Ashbâh wa al-Naẓâ'ir*, pp. 300–301; al-Fayrûzabâdî, *Baṣâ'ir Dhawî al-Tamyîz*, 5:413–21; Ibn al-Jawzî, *Nuzhat al-Aʿyun al-Nawâẓir*, 2:230–31; Ibn Manẓûr, *Lisân al-ʿArab*, 12:649–52; Lane, *Arabic-English Lexicon*, p. 3064; Majmaʿ al-Lughat al-ʿArabiyya, *Muʿjam Alfâẓ al-Qur'ân al-Karîm*, pp. 753–55; Mûsâ, *Qâmûs Qur'ânî*, pp. 221–22; Muṣṭafâ, *al-Muʿjam al-Wasîṭ*, p. 1067; al-Zabîdî, *Tâj al-ʿArûs*, 9:115; al-Zamakhsharî, *Asâs al-Balâgha*, p. 514.

9. *Dîn: Judgment*

DÎN (دين): From the Arabic root, د ي ن . ***Dîn*** is a comprehensive Quranic term, the meaning of which extends to four areas: (1) Religion in general and, more specifically, *the* religion (*al-dîn*), namely, Islam; (2) obedience, submission, and adherence to faith in Allah and His Revelation; (3) recompense or requital with regard to reward or punishment; and (4) economic transactions.

Dîn is often rendered as "religion." Its Quranic usage, however, covers a wide range of meanings, comprehending even those religions that the Quran regards as invalid or based on false assumptions and beliefs. The Quran says, for instance, *For you is your "religion," and for me is my "religion"* (109:6). Yet in other usages in the Quran, *dîn* certainly denotes Islam, either by name (3:85) or by direct or general inference, such as the expressions *dîn Allâh,* Allah's religion (3:83, 24:2, 110:2); *dîn al-ḥaqq*, the true religion (9:29, 33); *al-dîn al-qayyim,* the upright religion (9:36; 12:40; 30:30, 43; 98:5); *al-dîn al-khâliṣ*, the pure religion (39:3); and the religion pleasing to Allah (5:3). Also, *dîn* implies Islam in the statement, *There is no compulsion in religion* (2:256).

In somewhat extended usage, *dîn* implies the *Sharîᶜa*, Islam's guidance for the behavior of human beings as both individuals and members of society (42:13).

Dîn also means "judgment," connoting repayment or recompense, most strikingly when used as in the phrase *Yawm al-Dîn,* Day of Judgment. This usage occurs fourteen times in various Quranic contexts, such as people believing in (70:26) or denying the reality of that day (74:46, 83:11); expressing regret (37:20) or hoping for forgiveness (26:82); or, as is unique to al-Fâtiḥa, expressing Allah's absolute mastership and sovereignty over that day, *Mâlik Yawm al-Dîn* (1:4).

Another derivative mentioned in the Quran is *dayn*, meaning "debt," as in the case of a person who is under the obligation of payment for borrowing, purchasing, or being liable for something. It also refers to documentation and payment of debt-related transactions, as in the Quran's instructions to the believers to record in writing their loan arrangements, *tadâyantum* (2:282), or to pay bequests and debts prior to distributing shares of inheritance, as in the instruction that a husband honor bequests made by his deceased wife and meet her outstanding obligations before receiving his portion of her estate (4:11–12).

REFERENCES: ᶜAbd al-Bâqî, *al-Muᶜjam al-Mufahras*, pp. 267–69; al-Aṣfahânî, *al-Mufradât*, pp. 177–78; al-Balkhî, *al-Ashbâh wa al-Naẓâ'ir*, pp. 133–34; al-Fayrûzabâdî, *Baṣâ'ir Dhawî al-Tamyîz*, 2:615–17; Ibn al-Jawzî, *Nuzhat al-Aᶜyun al-Nawâẓir*, 1:184–88; Ibn Manẓûr, *Lisân al-ᶜArab*, 13:166–71; Ibn Qutayba al-Dînawarî, *Ta'wîl Mushkil al-Qur'ân*, pp. 453–54; Lane, *Arabic-English Lexicon*, 3:942–45; Majmaᶜ al-Lughat al-ᶜArabiyya, *Muᶜjam Alfâẓ al-Qur'ân al-Karîm*, p. 215; Mûsâ, *Qâmûs Qur'ânî*, pp. 144, 284–85; Muṣṭafâ, *al-Muᶜjam al-Wasîṭ*, p. 307; al-Sayyid, *al-Afᶜâl fî al-Qur'ân al-Karîm*, 1:510–11; al-Zabîdî, *Tâj al-ᶜArûs*, 9:207–9; al-Zamakhsharî, *Asâs al-Balâgha*, p. 140.

10. Naᶜbud: We worship

NAᶜBUD (نَعْبُدُ): From the Arabic root, ع ب د. ***Naᶜbud,*** the present-tense, first-person plural form, means "we worship." Its common nominal form, *ᶜibâda,* includes three elements: (1) Worship and adoration; (2) obedience and submission; and (3) devotion. It also connotes being easily led, handled, managed, or wrought. Interestingly, *ᶜabd* is also the name of a desert plant known for its pleasant fragrance and the love camels have for it, since it increases both their weight and milk. It is called *ᶜabd* because of the strong attraction and fondness it evokes, underscoring an important implication of the relationship between worship and love. Genuine worship is founded on will and choice. The more one reflects upon Allah's greatness and blessings, the greater the love and the stronger the desire to worship Him becomes.

ᶜIbâdatullâh (the worship of Allah) is not, therefore, an ordinary submission but a loving obedience to Allah, which includes none other than Him. The Quran proclaims that worshipping Allah—adoring Him, obeying Him, and submitting to Him—is the principal objective of life for which people were created (51:56). To every community a messenger has been sent calling people to worship Allah and to shun evil (16:36), a mandate constituting their very mission.

Thus, worship is the wellspring of good behavior and motives, as long as it stems from sincere devotion to Allah alone and is performed with steadfastness, through hardship and ease, until the end of one's life (15:99, 19:65). The Quran instructs the Prophet ﷺ to declare openly that he is commanded to worship Allah sincerely, for the religion is that which is practiced with pure devotion to God (39:2, 11, 14; 98:5). Submission to all else—idols, angels, jinn, humans, celestial bodies, clergy, sects, stones, whims, deviant dictates of society, and so forth—is characterized by the Quran as fruitless.

The Quran records David and Jesus, peace be upon them, condemning the violation of God's commandments and the neglect of essential religious performance by the disbelievers among the Children of Israel (5:78), stating also that the disbelievers among the People of the Book splintered into sects on the basis of doctrinal differences, though they were charged with no more than upholding sincere "worship" to God, to whom belongs the upright religion (98:4–5).

A final distinguishing feature of worship is the protection it offers one from evil, for whoever sincerely worships Allah is safe from Satan's dominion (15:42).

REFERENCES: ʿAbd al-Bâqî, *al-Muʿjam al-Mufahras*, pp. 441–45; Abû ʿÛda, *al-Taṭawwur al-Dalâlî*, pp. 140–46; al-Aṣfahânî, *al-Mufradât*, pp. 330–31; al-Balkhî, *al-Ashbâh wa al-Naẓâ'ir*, p. 288; al-Fayrûzabâdî, *Baṣâ'ir Dhawî al-Tamyîz*, 4:8–13; Ibn al-Jawzî, *Nuzhat al-Aʿyun al-Nawâẓir*, 2:45–46; Ibn Manẓûr, *Lisân al-ʿArab*, 3:270–79; Lane, *Arabic-English Lexicon*, 5:1934–36; Majmaʿ al-Lughat al-ʿArabiyya, *Muʿjam Alfâẓ al-Qur'ân al-Karîm*, pp. 406–8; Mûsâ, *Qâmûs Qur'ânî*, p. 191; Muṣṭafâ, *al-Muʿjam al-Wasîṭ*, pp. 579–80; al-Sayyid, *al-Afʿâl fî al-Qur'ân al-Karîm*, 2:891–93; al-Zabîdî, *Tâj al-ʿArûs*, 2:409–14; al-Zamakhsharî, *Asâs al-Balâgha*, pp. 291–92.

11. Nastaʿîn: We ask for help

NASTAʿÎN (نَسْتَعِين): From the Arabic root, ع و ن. ***Nastaʿîn*** (first person plural) is derived from the word *ʿawn* (or *ʿuwn*), which means to help or give aid, assistance, support, or cooperation. But when the reflexive Arabic particle "*ist*" (or "*nast*" in this case) is prefixed to it, it means the act of asking, seeking, or utilizing the help of someone or something in order to achieve an end or perform a desired or required task.

The derivative *ʿawân* is used to describe a beast, such as a cow (or a horse), that is neither young nor old (2:68); a tall palm tree; or the capacity to stand independent of others. It further describes the capacity to wage successive wars. Similarly, *aʿâna*, from the same root, means protection given to one by a tribe, a community, or a strong individual. Thus, an underlying meaning of the derivatives of this root is power, vigor, or zeal.

In the Quranic context, *ᶜawn*, appearing eleven times in variant forms, is used three times to indicate human aid, as when believers are commanded to join together to do what is right for the common good and to avoid wrongdoing and aggression (5:2); when Dhû'l-Qarnayn requests a work force to fulfill the need of those who "sought his help" (18:95); and when the disbelievers allege that the Quran was forged and that other people "helped" in its forgery (25:4).

When found in the form *istiᶜâna*, as in al-Fâtiḥa (1:5), the help sought is from Allah. He commanded Muslims (2:153), as He did the Children of Israel (2:45), to seek His help through patience and Prayer (*Ṣalât*). When Pharaoh passed the death sentence on the male offspring of the Children of Israel and decreed the holding of their women in bondage, Moses instructed them to seek Allah's help and be patient, promising them that ultimate victory is for those who fear God (7:128). Also, Jacob reaffirmed his reliance on the source of assistance and relief when his sons related to him that their brother Joseph fell prey to a wolf (12:18). Prophet Muḥammad, peace be upon him, sought help from his all-merciful Lord against what the disbelievers of Quraysh falsely ascribed to Allah and His Messenger and their denial of His message (21:112).

REFERENCES: ᶜAbd al-Bâqî, *al-Muᶜjam al-Mufahras*, p. 494; al-Aṣfahânî, *al-Mufradât*, p. 366; al-Fayrûzabâdî, *Baṣâ'ir Dhawî al-Tamyîz*, 4:113; Ibn Manẓûr, *Lisân al-ᶜArab*, 13:298–301; Lane, *Arabic-English Lexicon*, 5:2203–4; Majmaᶜ al-Lughat al-ᶜArabiyya, *Muᶜjam Alfâẓ al-Qur'ân al-Karîm*, pp. 445–46; Muṣṭafâ, *al-Muᶜjam al-Wasîṭ*, p. 641; al-Sayyid, *al-Afᶜâl fî al-Qur'ân al-Karîm*, 2:976–77;

al-Zabîdî, *Tâj al-ʿArûs,* 9:285–86; al-Zamakhsharî, *Asâs al-Balâgha,* pp. 317–18.

12. *Ihdinâ: Guide us*

IHDINÂ (اِهْدِنَا): From the Arabic root, ه د ي . ***Ihdinâ,*** "guide us," from the infinitive *hudâ,* means "right guidance," especially in the religious sense. It also denotes leading someone or something to the right way or true religion. The word *hudâ* itself occurs seventy-nine times in the Quran, with different forms occurring 237 times. Only twice does it come in the petition form *ihdinâ,* in al-Fâtiḥa (1:6) and in Sûrat Ṣâd (38:22), both usages referring to seeking guidance to the straight way.

Hudâ is the opposite of *ḍalâl,* error or misguidance. It occurs primarily in reference to following the revealed religion, namely, Islam. Its basic meaning, however, is highly nuanced. In the Quranic context, *hudâ* most often means to give proper direction, thereby removing confusion, or to identify or lead one through the unknown to an objective or destination. Allah asks rhetorically, *Who "guides" you through the darkness of land and sea. . . ?* (27:63). But while its basic usage strongly implies a movement toward an ultimate good, *hudâ* is used elsewhere in the Quran satirically to mean "leading" those who rejected guidance during their lifetime along the path to Hell in the Hereafter (37:23).

In another usage, however, *hudâ* refers to what God has given to His prophets and believers, including the revelation of Books (2:2), namely, the "guidance" ordaining the way of life and system of belief which the prophets called people to, thus forming the essence of their mission. This underscores another connotation of *hudâ* that refers to an individual worthy to be followed or emulated as a guiding model. In this sense, it describes the common principles and moral character of the prophets and the righteous (6:90). In somewhat extended usage, Allah's guidance is that which inspires the flowering and functioning of inherent gifts, talents, and genius in all creation, especially in human beings, as in Moses' answer to Pharaoh, *Our Lord is He who gives everything form, then "guides" it* (20:50), or in another verse, *[He] determines it and "guides" it* (87:3). Affixing the definite article "*al*" to *hudâ* makes it a synonym for the straight way, the upright religion, or the person (usually a prophet) calling and leading people to truth.

In relation to believers, *hudâ* is the continued affirmation of their life's course, coupled with evolving comprehension, maturing devotion, and fulfillment of Allah's will to achieve success in this world and the next (43:27). The word *ihtadâ'* refers to recognizing guidance, adding to *hudâ* the meaning of upholding and submitting to the articles of faith (2:137). As for *hudâ,* in the sense of actually "guiding" people to faith, this shade of the word strictly denotes Allah's will, for *He "guides" whomever He wills to the straight way* (2:142, 213). Moreover, the Quran records the supplication in which worshippers ask Allah not to allow their hearts to swerve after He has guided them (3:8). From this meaning, it is not difficult to understand how one of this root's basic indications is *hadiyya*, a "gift" of value that is freely given to honor or favor another (27:36). Also *hady*, an "offering," refers to that which is sacrificed (that is, animals permitted as food, such as cows, sheep, camels, and so on) during the Pilgrimage for consumption and distribution among the needy (2:196, 5:97, 48:25).

REFERENCES: ᶜAbd al-Bâqî, *al-Muᶜjam al-Mufahras*, pp. 731–36; Abû ᶜÛda, *al-Taṭawwur al-Dalâlî*, pp. 319–22; al-Aṣfahânî, *al-Mufradât*, pp. 536–39; al-Balkhî, *al-Ashbâh wa al-Naẓâ'ir*, pp. 89–95; al-Fayrûzabâdî, *Baṣâ'ir Dhawî al-Tamyîz*, 5:312–19; Ibn al-ᶜImâd, *Kashf al-Sarâ'ir*, pp. 26–32; Ibn al-Jawzî, *Nuzhat al-Aᶜyun al-Nawâẓir*, 2:221–26; Ibn Manẓûr, *Lisân al-ᶜArab*, 15:353–60; Ibn Qutayba al-Dînawarî, *Ta'wîl Mushkil al-Qur'ân*, pp. 443–44; Lane, *Arabic-English Lexicon*, 8:3042; Majmaᶜ al-Lughat al-ᶜArabiyya, *Muᶜjam Alfâẓ al-Qur'ân al-Karîm*, pp. 694–99; Mûsâ, *Qâmûs Qur'ânî*, pp. 40, 137, 395–98; al-Sayyid, *al-Afᶜâl fî al-Qur'ân al-Karîm*, 3:1401–5; al-Zabîdî, *Tâj al-ᶜArûs*, 10:406–9; al-Zamakhsharî, *Asâs al-Balâgha*, pp. 481–82.

13. Ṣirâṭ: Way

ṢIRÂṬ (صراط): From the Arabic root, ص ر ط. ***Ṣirâṭ***, literally, is a paved path, road, or way meant for traveling to a specific destination, free of obstructions, twists, and bends. This concrete application is used in the Quran, as when Prophet Shuᶜayb appeals to his people to cease ambushing travelers along "the road," although some interpret this metaphorically (7:86).

Nevertheless, in its forty-five occurrences, it is the figurative usage of *ṣirâṭ* to which the Quran most often alludes, usually qualifying it by some attribute of spiritual dimension, as in *Ṣirâṭillâh*, the Way of God (42:53); *Ṣirâṭi-Rabbik*, the Way of Your Lord (6:126); *Ṣirâṭ'l-Jaḥîm*, the Way of the Flame (37:23); and *Ṣirâṭî*, My (Allah's) Way (6:153).

The Quran refers to the straight way as the path of all the prophets, culminating in that of Muḥammad ﷺ. *Indeed, you call them to the straight way* (23:73). Abraham was *guided to the straight way* (16:122), and he said to his father, *Follow me; I will guide you to the straight way* (19:43). Likewise, Jesus, the son of Mary, called his people to worship their one Lord, saying, *My Lord is your Lord. So worship Him. This is the straight way* (19:36). Among the Quran's commandments is to adhere to this straight way, shunning all other paths, for they lead to division (6:153). *Ṣirâṭ* also refers to an overpass above Hell (*Jahannam*), which each individual will have to cross to enter Heaven.

REFERENCES: ʿAbd al-Bâqî, *al-Muʿjam al-Mufahras*, p. 407; Abû ʿÛda, *al-Taṭawwur al-Dalâlî*, pp. 464–67; al-Aṣfahânî, *al-Mufradât*, pp. 235–36, 287; al-Balkhî, *al-Ashbâh wa al-Naẓâ'ir*, p. 289; al-Fayrûzabâdî, *Baṣâ'ir Dhawî al-Tamyîz*, 3:411; Ibn al-Jawzî, *Nuzhat al-Aʿyun al-Nawâẓir*, 2:2; Ibn Manẓûr, *Lisân al-ʿArab*, 7:340; Lane, *Arabic-English Lexicon*, 4:1348–49, 4:1678; Majmaʿ al-Lughat al-ʿArabiyya, *Muʿjam Alfâẓ al-Qur'ân al-Karîm*, pp. 354–55; Mûsâ, *Qâmûs Qur'ânî*, pp. 191, 445; Muṣṭafâ, *al-Muʿjam al-Wasîṭ*, p. 512; al-Zabîdî, *Tâj al-ʿArûs*, 5:174; al-Zamakhsharî, *Asâs al-Balâgha*, p. 208.

14. *Mustaqîm: Straight [way]*

MUSTAQÎM (مُستَقِيم): From the Arabic root, ق و م . The literal and figurative meanings of this root revolve around the notion of rising, standing erect, straightness, or evenness. It also connotes a sense of integrity in constitution or composition, or freedom from crookedness or deviation.

The basic meaning of the derivative form *qiyâm* is to draw up one's physical stature to its full, upright length, as in a standing posture. A person having risen from reclining, sitting, or bowing to a standing position is called *qâ'im*. Another application of *qâ'im* or *qâma* is a turning wheel used to draw water from a well.

Something is said to be *mustaqîm* when it is straight or when it proceeds to a destination without obstruction. A person is described as *mustaqîm* when in motives, statements, and actions—and under varying conditions—he or she adheres to a path of goodness, upholding truth or justice, or is in a correct or right state, or continues along the right way without deviating. A road is said to be *mustaqîm* when it is even or direct, or if it takes one in the right direction or toward the desired point.

The Quran is described as a reminder for those who resolve to be "straight" (81:28). The Prophet, peace be upon him, was instructed to proclaim that God is one and that people should "go straight" on His path and seek His forgiveness (41:6). Those who say, *Our Lord is Allah,* and hold to the "straight" way are promised freedom from fear and grief in this life, and are promised Paradise in the Hereafter (41:30, 46:13–14). Believers are commanded to "be straight" even with their adversaries as long as the latter are "straight" regarding their pacts (9:7).

A variety of literal and figurative applications stemming from this root appear elsewhere in the Quran. The usages of the intransitive forms generally denote a standing or upright posture. The Quran says that the human condition is such that when harm touches people, they implore their Lord reclining, sitting, and "standing" (10:12). The Quran also refers to "standing" for Prayer *(Ṣalât)* in a mosque that is founded on devotion to God (9:108). Another reference is made to those who, for trade or other diversions, left the Prophet ﷺ "standing" in Prayer (62:11). Also, the Quran instructed the Prophet ﷺ never to pray over any of the hypocrites nor to "stand" over their graves (9:84).

The word *qâma* also means simply to stand still or stop, as in the Quran's reference to the parable of the hypocrites, who are like people in the midst of a storm, moving when lightning illumines the way and "standing still" when darkness again overtakes them (2:20).

In another usage, the verb *qâma* indicates resolving to do something and then proceeding to achieve it. The believers, for example, are required to make ablution when they "resolve" to stand for the Prayer (5:6). In a similar usage, the Quran notes that when the hypocrites "rise" to pray they "stand" lazily for prayer without real interest, just to be seen by people (4:142).

Another application indicates the realization or happening of something. The Quran records Abraham asking his Lord to forgive him, his parents, and the believers on the day when the Reckoning "takes place" (14:41).

The derivative *qiyâm* applies to undertaking, executing, performing, or watching over something. The Quran, for example, commands Muslims to "uphold" justice with orphans, that is, to be fair in administering their affairs and guarding their interests (4:127).

Some of the transitive usages of this root connote taking up residence or staying in a place (16:80, 25:76, 33:13). Related to this is the established performance of religious obligations, for without fulfilling the revealed commandments one cannot claim adherence to divine guidance. Thus the Prophet ﷺ was instructed to say to the People of the Book that they "stand" upon nothing unless they establish and perform all that is in the Torah and the Gospel and whatever has been sent down to them from their Lord (2:229, 5:68, 98:5). This usage stresses vigilance and observance of God's commandments. Also, the Quran repeatedly commands believers to "establish" Prayer (*Ṣalât*), give Charity *(Zakât)*, and obey Allah and His Messenger (24:56, 33:33, 58:13). Derived from the same root is *qiyâma*, a word describing the resurrection of human beings from their graves to stand for final judgment before God (75:1, 6).

The word *qawm*, also from this root, means a people, community, company, party, or group of men and women. An example is Joseph's statement, *I have forsaken the ways of a "people" who do not believe in Allah* (12:37), or when the Quran instructs believers not to permit the ridicule of one people by another (49:11). One of Allah's attributes, *al-Qayyûm*, is an intensive form derived from the same root, meaning "the Self-Subsisting," the One by whom all creation subsists (2:255).

The phrase *al-ṣirâṭ al-mustaqîm*, "the straight way," appears twenty-eight times in the Quran. Basically, this is the path, ethos, norm, morality, affirmation of belief, and direction of the rightly guided—the way of those upon whom Allah has bestowed grace. It is their blessed ways and practices that worshippers ask for in the central prayer of al-Fâtiḥa, that is, the straight way of living based on revealed guidance, not the *ṣirâṭ* of those upon whom there is wrath, nor the way of those who have gone astray (1:5). But the Quran makes it clear that Satan can be an obstacle lurking on the straight way, tempting and luring people away from it (7:16). But whosoever holds firmly to what Allah has revealed is guided upon His straight way (3:101).

Quranic authorities define *al-ṣirâṭ al-mustaqîm* as a phrase that implies Islam, the Quran, the middle way between extremes, or moderation in character, ideas, and actions. In essence, *al-ṣirâṭ al-mustaqîm* is the shortest distance to eternal salvation. It leads to the final destination; it accommodates everyone willing to proceed on it; it is accessible to every traveler; and it is the way Allah has specified, commending those who have adhered to it, who are pleased with it, and with whom He is pleased.

REFERENCES: ʿAbd al-Bâqî, *al-Muʿjam al-Mufahras*, pp. 578–87; Abû ʿÛda, *al-Taṭawwur al-Dalâlî*, pp. 362–64; al-Aṣfahânî, *al-Mufradât*, pp. 431–34; al-Balkhî, *al-Ashbâh wa al-Naẓâ'ir*, pp. 139, 313–14; al-Fayrûzabâdî, *Baṣâ'ir Dhawî al-Tamyîz*, 4:307–13; Ibn al-Jawzî, *Nuzhat al-Aʿyun al-Nawâẓir*, 2:108–10; Ibn Manẓûr, *Lisân al-ʿArab*, 12:496–506; Lane, *Arabic-English Lexicon*, 8:2995–97; Majmaʿ al-Lughat al-ʿArabiyya, *Muʿjam Alfâẓ al-Qur'ân al-Karîm*, pp. 530–37; Mûsâ, *Qâmûs Qur'ânî*, pp. 191, 445; Muṣṭafâ, *al-Muʿjam al-Wasîṭ*, pp. 767–68; al-Sayyid, *al-Afʿâl fî al-Qur'ân al-Karîm*, 3:1143–48; al-Zabîdî, *Tâj al-ʿArûs*, 9:34–38; al-Zamakhsharî, *Asâs al-Balâgha*, p. 382.

15. *Niʿma [Anʿamta]: Grace*

NIʿMA (نعمة): From the Arabic root, ن ع م . ***Niʿma,*** originally referring to that which is soft, tender, smooth, or easy, generally denotes a benefit, favor, good, or blessing that is imparted to a person or community, that is, the bestowal of grace. In Quranic usage, every *niʿma* (pl. *niʿam*) flows from Allah; for good comes only from Him (16:53). Hence, *niʿma* implies Allah's bestowal of grace, favor, and blessings upon creation. Its meaning is not limited to what is tangible, for it also denotes a shield from harm. The Quran reminded the early Muslims in Madinah to *remember Allah's "grace"* in saving them from the massive siege led by the disbelieving Quraysh (33:9). Thus the meaning of *niʿma* includes all the material and spiritual good that reaches and benefits humans in this life and the next, for *naʿîm* (a derivative of *niʿma*) also describes the *"delighting" Garden* in the life to come (56:89). Allah's blessings upon people are to be cherished, for there is no creator besides Allah to bestow sustenance from the sky and the earth (35:3) as well as countless gifts to creation, such as life, arable land, water resources, plants, and animals to enjoy, ease toil, and provide nourishment (14:34). These favors of Allah reflect His mercy and forgiveness (16:18). In fact, His blessings, visible and invisible, are so extensive that the Quran states He showers them upon creation (31:20).

Allah bestows His blessings especially upon people who are conscious of Him and are vigilant regarding the welfare of their community (5:23). Among the manifestations of Allah's grace is that He raised from among various communities prophets and messengers to guide and warn them (5:20, 19:58). Thus people are obliged to express gratitude to Allah for bestowing His grace upon them, as in the instruction to eat of the wholesome and permissible things and to be thankful for His blessings (16:114). Allah continues His favor upon people as long as they are steadfast in worshipping Him (8:53) and are mindful of obeying His commandments and honoring His covenant (5:7).

The Quran also exposes an all-too-common human response to Allah's blessings, as well as to His trials. When Allah grants blessings to people, some turn away and go adrift; yet when touched with calamity, they pray incessantly (41:51). Moreover, when relief comes, people often attribute it to their own doing, intelligence, or merit, neglecting to acknowledge their Lord's favors (17:83). The steadfast, however, turn to Allah, asking Him to enable them to be thankful for His grace upon them. Further, they are grateful on behalf of their parents and are hopeful for continued favors in the gift of children (27:19, 46:15). Perhaps Allah's greatest blessing upon humanity is the favor of the highest knowledge, namely, Revelation, as expressed in scripture and the teachings of its bearers (2:231), culminating in the final Revelation, the Quran (5:3).

REFERENCES: ʿAbd al-Bâqî, *al-Muʿjam al-Mufahras*, pp. 707–10; Abû ʿÛda, *al-Taṭawwur al-Dalâlî*, pp. 408–12; al-Aṣfahânî, *al-Mufradât*, pp. 520–21; al-Fayrûzabâdî, *Baṣâ'ir Dhawî al-Tamyîz*, 5:88–91; Ibn al-Jawzî, *Nuzhat al-Aʿyun al-Nawâẓir*, 2:194–95; Ibn Manẓûr, *Lisân al-ʿArab*, 12:579–90; Lane, *Arabic-English Lexicon*, 8:3035; Majmaʿ al-Lughat al-ʿArabiyya, *Muʿjam Alfâẓ al-Qur'ân al-Karîm*, pp. 669–71; Muṣṭafâ, *al-Muʿjam al-Wasîṭ*, pp. 935–36; al-Sayyid, *al-Afʿâl fî al-Qur'ân al-Karîm*, 3:1361–64; al-Zabîdî, *Tâj al-ʿArûs*, 9:77–83; al-Zamakhsharî, *Asâs al-Balâgha*, p. 464.

16. Maghḍûb: Wrath

MAGHḌÛB (مَغْضُوب): From the Arabic root, غ ض ب. ***Maghḍûb*** is derived from *ghaḍab*, which means wrath, indignation, or anger aroused by displeasure, suggesting grievance or intent to punish something or someone. Appearing in the Quran twenty-four times in various forms, the word *maghḍûb* occurs only in al-Fâtiḥa, as part of the phrase *those upon whom there is wrath.*

In referring to Allah's wrath, *ghaḍab* and its derivatives occur in the Quran mainly in six general contexts: (1) Deliberate violation of the covenant with Allah, which includes taking as patrons, or condoning the acts of, people upon whom His wrath has been explicitly stated, or those who disbelieve in Him (16:106, 60:13); (2) the deliberate slaying of a believer (4:93); (3) disobedience to or slaying of prophets, denying Allah's signs, and committing aggression (2:90, 3:112); (4) the desertion of the believers in battle (8:16); (5) excessive consumption or wastage of what Allah has provided (20:81); and (6) the invoking of Allah's wrath upon oneself, as a moral shield, when asserting that an accusation of infidelity is falsely claimed (24:8–9).

In variant forms, *ghaḍab* also applies to human beings, as in the "outrage" Moses expressed when the Israelites took to worshipping the golden calf (7:150, 154; 20:86), and with regard to Jonah's desperate "anger" over his community's indifference to his call (21:87).

The ability to overcome anger and forgive is cited by Allah as a distinguishing characteristic of a believer (42:37). Though human, and therefore susceptible to *ghaḍab*, people are encouraged to rise to the higher station of forgiveness, recovery, and patience. The Prophet, peace be upon him, said that might is not knocking down one's opponent, but in restraining oneself when angry.[43]

REFERENCES: ʿAbd al-Bâqî, *al-Muʿjam al-Mufahras*, p. 499; al-Aṣfahânî, *al-Mufradât*, p. 374; al-Fayrûzabâdî, *Baṣâ'ir Dhawî al-Tamyîz*, 4:135–36; Ibn Manẓûr, *Lisân al-ʿArab*, 1:648–51; Lane, *Arabic-English Lexicon*, 6:2265–66; Majmaʿ al-Lughat al-ʿArabiyya, *Muʿjam Alfâẓ al-Qur'ân al-Karîm*, p. 454; Muṣṭafâ, *al-Muʿjam al-Wasîṭ*, p. 654; al-Sayyid, *al-Afʿâl fî al-Qur'ân al-Karîm*, 2:991–92; al-Zabîdî, *Tâj al-ʿArûs*, 1:412–13; al-Zamakhsharî, *Asâs al-Balâgha*, p. 325.

17. Ḍâllîn: Those astray

ḌÂLLÎN (ضالّين): From the Arabic root, ض ل ل . ***Ḍâllîn*** (sing. *ḍâll*), derived from *ḍalâl* or *ḍalâlah*, denotes straying from a certain way or from what is right. The verb *ḍalla* means to disappear, vanish, or become unobservable; to be ruined; to forget; to be misguided, mistaken, or in error; to be deluded, confused, or lost. The transitive form, *aḍalla* or *ḍallala*, indicates causing someone or something to pursue something other than the right course.

In addition, the noun *iḍlâl* has two meanings: (1) Losing the right course or direction either by misjudgment or due to the obscurity of the course and (2) presenting misguidance or the wrong course in a favorable light.

A literal signification of the word *iḍlâl* describes water running unchanneled through trees or under rocks where sunlight does not penetrate. It also signifies burial, since a corpse is hidden in the earth, as when the disbelievers ask rhetorically, *When we "vanish" into the earth, shall we then be brought to life anew?* (32:10).

Ḍalâl and its derivatives occur 191 times in the Quran, with varied meanings, although they most commonly denote "deviation" or "misguidance," the most heinous expression of which is the worship of anything other than God (46:5). The Quran is explicit about the varied forms this error may take. Idolatry, for example, is called "clear misguidance" (*ḍalâl mubîn*), which is mentioned twenty times in the Quran. The term *ḍalâl baʿîd*, or "far astray" or "further astray," appears thirteen times and is used to denote joining partners with Allah, denying His angels, scriptures, prophets, or the Day of Judgment, and obstructing or resisting guidance upon Allah's Way. In al-Fâtiḥa, the word *ḍâllîn*, or *those astray*, refers mainly to those who have fallen into an error of belief, thus deviating from the straight way.

The term also connotes "loss" or "misplacement," as of an object or possession, shedding increased light on its usage in al-Fâtiḥa. *Those astray* were not born so or predisposed to misguidance, nor were their ancestors deprived of warning (35:24).[44] In effect, they lost a sense of the natural course of living in adherence to the Creator's way, as exemplified by His messengers and prophets. Entreating God for guidance to the way of those upon whom He has bestowed grace and to be kept away from the path of those who have strayed adds to the meaning of *ḍâllîn* a sense of willing and conscious departure. For just as it is vital that one treading the straight way know the qualities of the "people of grace," it is equally important that he or she recognize the characteristics of the people of "wrath" and those "astray," namely, those who willfully breach their covenant with God or attribute to Him what they have no knowledge of. The Prophet ﷺ explained that among the Children of Israel are examples of *those upon whom there is wrath,* because of their deliberate and repeated violation of the covenant with God, while *those astray* makes reference to Christians who ascribe to God and His prophets what He Himself did not authorize.

The prophets alerted their communities against "clear misguidance," as in the case of Abraham confronting his own father and his people (6:74). Yet those who rejected or resisted the call replied that the prophets themselves were in "clear misguidance," as was the case with Noah's people (7:60). Similarly, the Prophet Muḥammad ﷺ and the believers with him were accused by the wrongdoers of being "misguided" (83:32). Those who mocked at the Prophet and charged him with "misleading" them from their gods, however, will realize their misguidance when they face punishment (25:41–42). And the greatest losers, according to the Quran, are those who think they are doing good while their worldly efforts are in vain (18:104). But when cast into Hell's blazing fire, the disbelievers will regret rejecting the very warners they dismissed as being in "great error," *ḍalâl kabîr* (67:9).

Ḍalâl and its derivatives have other usages in the Quran: Moses describes his Lord to Pharaoh as being free from "error" (20:52); Jacob is wrongfully accused by members of his household as persisting in his "old delusions," *ḍalâl qadîm* (12:95); and the Quran clarifies and details the rules of inheritance so that people may not be confused or "misguided" (4:176).

The prime seducer of people into error is Satan, whose enmity for Adam and his offspring is made clear in the Quran (12:5). His goal is to lead people astray; his method is deception. He has help among the human ranks, often through the influential and powerful who mislead their people, as did Pharaoh (20:79). Idols and alleged intermediaries are also sources of deception for many people (14:36).

Allah knows best who is astray and who is guided (53:30, 68:7). And He guides or leaves to stray whomever He wills (16:93, 35:8, 74:31). For He has made humans creatures of habit, such that our nature acquires an affinity for what it grows accustomed to and what it is intimate with—good or bad—to the extent that changing habitual behavior and thought becomes a monumental task.

It is a Quranic axiom, however, that *whomever Allah guides*, none can lead astray (39:37), and whomever Allah leaves to stray, *none can guide* (18:17). Following Allah's revealed guidance shields against deviation and misery

(20:123). Those who accept it do so for their own benefit, and those who stray from it do so at their own loss.

REFERENCES: ʿAbd al-Bâqî, *al-Muʿjam al-Mufahras*, pp. 421–24; Abû ʿÛda, *al-Taṭawwur al-Dalâlî*, pp. 319–22; al-Aṣfahânî, *al-Mufradât*, pp. 306–8; al-Balkhî, *al-Ashbâh wa al-Naẓâ'ir*, pp. 217–18; al-Fayrûzabâdî, *Baṣâ'ir Dhawî al-Tamyîz*, 3:481–85; Ibn al-Jawzî, *Nuzhat al-Aʿyun al-Nawâẓir*, 2:22–25; Ibn Manẓûr, *Lisân al-ʿArab*, 11:390–96; Lane, *Arabic-English Lexicon*, 5:1796–99; Majmaʿ al-Lughat al-ʿArabiyya, *Muʿjam Alfâẓ al-Qur'ân al-Karîm*, pp. 376–79; Muṣṭafâ, *al-Muʿjam al-Wasîṭ*, pp. 542–43; al-Sayyid, *al-Afʿâl fî al-Qur'ân al-Karîm*, 2:843–47; al-Zabîdî, *Tâj al-ʿArûs*, 7:410–14; al-Zamakhsharî, *Asâs al-Balâgha*, p. 271.

6

NOTES

1. Muslim ibn al-Ḥajjâj, *Ṣaḥîḥ*, 5 vols. (Beirut: Dâr al-Fikr, 1978), 1:296.

2. The Prophet's instruction to say "*Âmîn*" after reciting al-Fâtiḥa is reported in *Ṣaḥîḥ Muslim*, 1:310. See the discussion regarding the saying of "*Âmîn*" in "Rules of al-Fâtiḥa" (p. 30).

3. Jalâluddîn ʿAbd al-Raḥmân Abû Bakr al-Suyûṭî, *al-Itqân fî ʿUlûm al-Qur'ân*, ed. Muḥammad Abû al-Faḍl Ibrâhîm, 3d ed., 4 vols. (Cairo: Dâr al-Turâth, 1985), 1:72. See also Badruddîn al-Zarkashî, *al-Burhân fî ʿUlûm al-Qur'ân*, ed. Muḥammad Abû al-Faḍl Ibrâhîm, 3d ed., 4 vols. (n.p.: Dâr al-Fikr, 1980), 1:207; Aḥmad ibn Ḥajar al-ʿAsqalânî, *Fatḥ al-Bârî bi Sharḥ Ṣaḥîḥ al-Bukhârî*, 13 vols. (Riyâḍ: Maktabat al-Riyâḍ al-Ḥadîtha, n.d.), 8:676, 678, and 718; and Abû Bakr Aḥmad ibn al-Ḥusayn ibn ʿAlî al-Bayhaqî, *al-Sunan al-Kubrâ*, 10 vols. (Hyderabad: Maṭbûʿât Dâ'ira al-Maʿârif ʿUthmâniyya, reproduced by Beirut: Dâr al-Maʿrifa, 1347 H).

4. Al-Suyûṭî, *al-Itqân fî ʿUlûm al-Qur'ân*, 1:70.

5. *Ṣaḥîḥ al-Bukhârî*, 1:23. See also al-Suyûṭî, *al-Itqân fî ʿUlûm al-Qur'ân*, 1:70–71.

6. For a survey of the various opinions concerning the chronology of al-Fâtiḥa's revelation, see al-Zarkashî, *al-Burhân fî ʿUlûm al-Qur'ân*, 1:207. Abû al-Ḥajjâj Mujâhid ibn Jabr (d. 104/722), a Makkan scholar who studied under ʿAlî ibn Abî Ṭâlib, Ibn ʿAbbâs, and ʿUbay ibn Kaʿb, stated that al-Fâtiḥa was revealed in Madinah. For his opinion, see al-Suyûṭî, *al-Durr al-Manthûr fî al-Tafsîr bi al-Ma'thûr* (Beirut: Dâr al-Fikr, 1983), 1:11.

7. Aḥmad ibn ʿAlî ibn Shuʿayb al-Nasâ'î, *Sunan al-Nasâ'î*, 8 vols. (Beirut: Dâr al-Kitâb al-ʿArabî, n.d.), 2:138.

8. For a full account of the names and the meanings of al-Fâtiḥa, see Abû Jaʿfar Muḥammad ibn Jarîr al-Ṭabarî, *Jâmiʿ al-Bayân ʿan Ta'wîl Ây al-Qur'ân*, 3d ed., 30 vols. (in twelve) (Cairo: Al-Ḥalabî Press, 1968), 1:47–49. See also Abû ʿAbdullâh Muḥammad ibn Aḥmad al-Anṣârî al-Qurṭubî, *al-Jamiʿ li Aḥkâm al-Qur'ân*, 2d ed., 20 vols. (Cairo: Dâr al-Kutub al-Miṣriyya, 1952–1967), 1:111–14; Majduddîn Muḥammad ibn Yaʿqûb al-Fayrûzabâdî, *Baṣâ'ir Dhawî al-Tamyîz*, edited by Muḥammad ʿAlî al-Najjâr, 8 vols. (Beirut: Maktaba al-ʿIlmiyya, n.d.), 1:128–32; and Shihâbuddîn al-Sayyid Maḥmûd al-Alûsî, *Rûḥ al-Maʿânî fî Tafsîr al-Qur'ân al-Aẓîm wa Sabʿ al-Mathânî*, 30 vols. (in fifteen) (Cairo: Ṭabaʿa al-Munîriyya, 1353/1934).

9. Al-Nasâ'î, *ʿAmal al-Yawm wa al-Layla*, p. 345, #494. See also ʿImâduddîn Ismâʿîl ibn Kathîr, *Tafsîr al-Qur'ân al-ʿAẓîm*, 4 vols. (Egypt: ʿÎsâ al-Bâbî al-Ḥalabî, n.d.), 1:18; and ʿAlâ'uddîn ʿAlî al-Muttaqqî ibn Ḥusâmuddîn al-Hindî, *Kanz al-ʿUmmâl fî Sunan al-Aqwâl wa al-Afʿâl*, 15 vols. (Beirut: Mu'assasat al-Risâla, 1979), 1:555, 558.

The *ḥadîth* literature is rich with contexts in which the Prophet ﷺ invoked the name of Allah. For example, he said, "There is no ablution for whoever does not mention the name of Allah before it" (*Sunan al-Tirmidhî*, 1:37–39, #25, 26, and *Sunan al-Nasâ'î*, 1:61). In seeking refuge against harm, the Prophet ﷺ would say three times, "In the name of Allah, with whose name nothing can be harmed in the earth nor in the heavens. He is the All-Hearing, the All-Knowing" (*Sunan al-Tirmidhî,* 5:434, #3388). Before sleeping, he would say, "In the name of Allah, I lay my side down. O Allah, forgive me my sins and impel away my devil and release my debts and place me among the highest assembly" (*Sunan Abû Dâwûd,* 4:313, #5054). For other occasions, see my work *Lasting Prayers of the Quran and the Prophet Muḥammad* ﷺ.

10. Al-Ṭabarî, *Jâmiʿ al-Bayân ʿan Ta'wîl Ây al-Qur'ân,* 1:59.

11. Al-Qurṭubî, *al-Jamiʿ li Aḥkâm al-Qur'ân,* 1:34.

12. Aḥmad ibn Ḥanbal, *Musnad al-Imâm Aḥmad,* 6 vols. (Beirut: Al-Maktab al-Islâmî, 1969), 2:258. Though worded differently, the same meaning of this *ḥadîth* is expressed in two other reports, *Musnad Aḥmad,* 2:295, 303.

13. *Ṣaḥîḥ Muslim,* 1:532–33.

14. *Ṣaḥîḥ Muslim,* 4:2108.

15. See also verses 29:19 and 50:44.

16. Abû Bakr Muḥammad ibn ʿAbdullâh ibn al-ʿArabî, *Aḥkâm al-Qur'ân,* ed. ʿAlî Muḥammad al-Bijâwî, 2 vols. (n.p.: Dâr al-Fikr, n.d.), 1:5.

17. Ibn Ḥajar al-ʿAsqalânî, *Fatḥ al-Bârî bi Sharḥ Ṣaḥîḥ al-Bukhârî,* 11:97–98.

18. *Ṣaḥîḥ Muslim,* 4:1994–95.

19. *Ṣaḥîḥ Muslim,* 2:1020.

20. *Musnad al-Imâm Aḥmad,* 1:391.

21. Al-Nasâ'î reported on good authority that Muʿâdh ibn Jabal said, "The Messenger of Allah ﷺ took my hand and said, 'I do love you, Muʿâdh.' So I said, 'I, too, love you, Messenger of Allah.' He said, 'Then never fail to say after each prayer, "O Allah, help me in always remembering You, and being thankful to You, and worshipping You in the most excellent way."'" See *Sunan al-Nasâ'î*, 3:53.

22. Muḥammad ibn ʿUmar al-Zamakhsharî, *al-Kashshâf ʿan Ḥaqâ'iq Ghawâmiḍ al-Tanzîl wa ʿUyûn al-Aqâwîl fî Wujûh al-Ta'wîl*, 4 vols. (Beirut: Dâr al-Maʿrifa, 1947; rpt., n.d.), 1:66.

23. Ibn Kathîr, *Tafsîr al-Qur'ân al-Aẓîm*, 4 vols. (n.p.: Dâr al-Fikr, n.d.), 1:28.

24. *Musnad al-Imâm Aḥmad*, 4:183.

25. See *Musnad Aḥmad*, 4:378–79, and *Ṣaḥîḥ al-Bukhârî*, 8:159. See also al-Ṭabarî who states that anyone "who turns away from [God's] way and follows other than the upright course is considered, in Arabic usage, one who has strayed." See *Jâmiʿ al-Bayân fî Tafsîr al-Qur'ân*, 1:115.

26. Ibn Ḥajar al-ʿAsqalânî, *Fatḥ al-Bârî bi Sharḥ Ṣaḥîḥ al-Bukhârî*, 1:158. The text is also found in *Ṣaḥîḥ Muslim*, 3:1305–6, with some variation.

27. The *ḥadîth* was reported by the Prophet's wife Umm Salama, who said that she always heard the Prophet ﷺ repeating these words as he left his home, turning his "face to the heavens." See Abû Dâwûd Sulaymân ibn al-Ashʿath, *Sunan Abû Dâwûd*, 4 vols. (in two) (n.p.: Dâr al-Fikr, n.d.), 4:325. This *ḥadîth* is also recorded in *Musnad Aḥmad*, 6:318, with some variation. The text here is a combination of two prayers that the Prophet ﷺ used to say when departing from his home.

28. *Ṣaḥîḥ Muslim*, 1:295. Another report (*Ṣaḥîḥ Muslim*, 1:296) reads, "Whoever performs a Prayer *(Ṣalât)* without reciting in it *Umm al-Quran* (al-Fâtiḥa), it (the Prayer) is indeed incomplete."

29. This is the interpretation of the Mâlikî, Shâfiʿî, and other schools. Based on this, one is obligated to make up or complete a Prayer in which al-Fâtiḥa was not recited. See Ibn al-ʿArabî, *Aḥkâm al-Qur'ân*, 1:2–3.

30. This is the ruling of the Ḥanafî school.

31. Al-Qurṭubî, *al-Jâmiʿ li Aḥkâm al-Qur'ân*, 1:126. See also an excellent concise discussion on this subject by Muḥammad ibn ʿAlî al-Shawkânî in his *fiqhî* work *Nayl al-Awṭâr*, 9 vols. (Beirut: Dâr al-Jîl, 1973), 2:247–48.

32. The Prophet's instruction to say *"Âmîn"* after reciting al-Fâtiḥa is reported in *Ṣaḥîḥ Muslim*, 1:310.

33. *Ṣaḥîḥ Muslim*, 1:307.

34. *Ṣaḥîḥ Muslim*, 1:307. See also Ibn al-ʿArabî, *Aḥkâm al-Qur'ân*, 1:7.

35. See Kamâluddîn Muḥammad ibn al-Humâm's *Sharḥ Fatḥ al-Qadîr* (Beirut: Dâr Ṣâdir, n.d.), 1:207, and Burhânuddîn Abû al-Ḥasan al-Marghinânî, *al-Hidâyah*, 4 vols. (Beirut: Dâr Ṣâdir, n.d.), 1:204, printed in the margins of Ibn al-Humâm's *Sharḥ Fatḥ al-Qadîr.*

36. Ibn Ḥajar al-ʿAsqalânî, *Fatḥ al-Bârî bi Sharḥ Ṣaḥîḥ al-Bukhârî*, 9:54.

37. Ibn Ḥajar al-ʿAsqalânî, *Fatḥ al-Bârî bi Sharḥ Ṣaḥîḥ al-Bukhârî*, 9:54.

38. *Sunan Abû Dâwûd*, 1:304, #1173.

39. Abû Ḥâmid al-Ghazâlî, in *al-Mustaṣfâ min ᶜIlm al-Uṣûl*, 2 vols. (Bulâq, Egypt: Amîriyya Press, 1322–24/1905–7), pp. 102–3. Al-Ghazâlî says, "The *basmala* is a verse of the Quran. But whether or not it is the first verse of every sura is disputed. The inclination of al-Shâfiᶜî is that it is a verse of every sura, be it *'al-Ḥamd'* (Sûrat al-Fâtiḥa) or the rest of the suras. But it is, in the beginning of every sura, a verse by itself, or it is a verse with the first verse of those suras." See also Ibn Kathîr, *Tafsîr al-Qur'ân al-ᶜAẓîm*, 1:16, for a detailed discussion about the place of the *Basmala* in the suras. He says there is a consensus among scholars that it is part of Sûrat al-Naml, but they differ as to whether it is a part of every sura or part of the first verse. They also differ as to whether it is part of al-Fâtiḥa. See also al-Shawkânî's *Nayl al-Awṭâr*, 2:215–29, which has an excellent summary of the various positions regarding the *Basmala*. This issue will be discussed in greater detail in the commentary on verse 30 of Sûrat al-Naml.

40. Al-Ghazâlî, *The Ninety-Nine Beautiful Names of God*, translated by David B. Burrell and Nazih Daher (Cambridge: Islamic Texts Society, 1992), p. 51.

41. Al-Nasâ'î, *ᶜAmal al-Yawm wa al-Layla*, p. 345, #494. See also Ibn Kathîr, *Tafsîr al-Qur'ân al-ᶜAẓîm*, 1:18.

42. *Musnad Aḥmad*, 1:191.

43. *Ṣaḥîḥ Muslim*, 4:2014.

44. *And there has not been any community but that a warner was [sent] among them* (35:24).

7

BIBLIOGRAPHY

ʿAbd al-Bâqî, Muḥammad Fu'âd. *Al-Muʿjam al-Mufahras li Alfâẓ al-Qur'ân al-Karîm*. Cairo, 1378/1958.

ʿAbd al-Jabbâr al-Asadâbâdî, al-Qâḍî. *Mutashâbih al-Qur'ân*. 2 vols. Edited by ʿAdnân M. Zarzûr. Cairo: Dâr al-Turâth, 1969.

ʿAbd al-Raḥmân, ʿÂ'isha [Bint al-Shâṭi', pseud.]. *Al-Tafsîr al-Bayânî li al-Qur'ân al-Karîm*. 2 vols. Cairo: Dâr al-Maʿârif, n.d.

______. *Al-Aʿjâz al-Bayânî li al-Qur'ân wa Masâ'il Ibn al-Azraq*. 2d ed. Cairo: Dâr al-Maʿârif, 1987.

Abû Dâwûd. *Sunan*. 4 vols. 1934. Reprint. 4 vols. in 2. Damascus: Dâr al-Fikr, n.d.

Abû al-Futûḥ, Muḥammad Ḥusayn. *Qâ'ima Muʿjamiyya bi Alfâẓ al-Qur'ân al-Karîm wa Darajât Takrâriha*. Beirut: Maktabat Lubnân, 1990.

Abû Ḥayyân al-Tawḥîdî, Abû ʿAbdullâh Muḥammad ibn Yûsuf. *Al-Tafsîr al-Kabîr al-Musammâ bi al-Baḥr al-Muḥîṭ*. 8 vols. Riyâḍ: Maktabat wa Maṭâbiʿ al-Naṣr al-Ḥadîtha, n.d.

Abû al-Saʿûd, Muḥammad ibn Muḥammad al-ʿImâdî. *Tafsîr Abî al-Saʿûd* [or *Irshâd al-ʿAql al-Salîm ilâ Mazâyâ al-*

Qur'ân al-Karîm]. 9 vols. in 5. Beirut: Dâr Iḥyâ' al-Turâth al-ʿArabî, n.d.

Abû Shahba, Muḥammad ibn Muḥammad. *Al-Madkhal li Dirâsat al-Qur'ân al-Karîm*. Beirut: Dâr al-Jîl, 1412/1992.

Abû ʿÛda, ʿÛda Khalîl. *Al-Taṭawwur al-Dalâlî bayna Lughat al-Shiʿr wa Lughat al-Qur'ân al-Karîm*. Zarqa, Jordan: Maktabat al-Manâr, 1985.

al-ʿAjlûnî, Ismâʿîl. *Kashf al-Khafâ' wa Muzîl al-Ilbâs ʿamma Ashtahara min al-Aḥâdîth ʿalâ Alsinat al-Nâs*. Edited by Aḥmad al-Qallâsh. 2 vols. Beirut: Mu'assasat al-Risâla, 1979.

al-Alûsî, Shihâbuddîn al-Sayyid Maḥmûd. *Rûḥ al-Maʿânî fî Tafsîr al-Qur'ân al-Aẓîm wa Sabʿ al-Mathânî*. 30 vols. in 15. Beirut: Dâr Iḥyâ' al-Turâth al-ʿArabî, 1353/1934.

ʿAmâyra, Ismâʿîl Aḥmad, and ʿAbd al-Ḥamîd Muṣṭafâ al-Sayyid. *Muʿjam al-Adawât wa al-Ḍamâ'ir fî al-Qur'ân al-Karîm*. Beirut: Mu'assasat al-Risâla, 1988.

al-Aṣfahânî, al-Râghib. *Al-Mufradât*. Beirut: Dâr al-Fikr, 1972.

al-Ashqar, Muḥammad Sulaymân ʿAbdullâh. *Zubdat al-Tafsîr min Fatḥ al-Qadîr*. Kuwait: Wazârat al-Awqâf, 1406/1985.

al-Balkhî, Muqâtil ibn Sulaymân. *Al-Ashbâh wa al-Naẓâ'ir fî al-Qur'ân al-Karîm*. Cairo: Al-Hay'a al-Miṣriyya, 1975.

al-Bayḍâwî, Nâṣiruddîn ʿAbdullâh ibn ʿUmar. *Anwâr al-Tanzîl wa Asrâr al-Ta'wîl* (or *Tafsîr al-Bayḍâwî*). 5 vols. in 2. Beirut: Mu'assasat Shaʿbân, n.d.

al-Bilâdî, ʿÂtiq ibn Ghayth. *Faḍâ'il al-Qur'ân*. Edited by Fârûq Ḥamâda. Makkah: Dâr Makkah, 1410/1990.

al-Biqâʿî [or al-Buqâʿî], Burhânuddîn Abû al-Ḥasan Ibrâhîm ibn ʿUmar. *Maṣâʿid al-Naẓar li al-Ishrâf ʿalâ Maqâṣid al-Suwar*. Edited by ʿAbd al-Samîʿ Muḥammad

Aḥmad Ḥasanayn. 3 vols. Riyâḍ: Maktabat al-Maᶜârif, 1987.

______. *Naẓm al-Durur fî Tanâsub al-Ayât wa al-Suwar*. 22 vols. Hyderabad: Maṭbûᶜât Dâ'ira al-Maᶜârif ᶜUthmâniyya (Osmania Oriental Publications Bureau), 1404/1984.

Darwaza, Muḥammad ᶜAzzat. *Al-Tafsîr al-Ḥadîth*. 12 vols. in 6. Cairo: ᶜÎsâ al-Bâbî al-Ḥalabî, n.d.

______. *Al-Dustûr al-Qur'ânî wa al-Sunna al-Nabawiyya*. 1966.

al-Darwîsh, Muḥîyuddîn. *Iᶜrâb al-Qur'ân al-Karîm wa Bayânuhu*. 3d ed. 10 vols. Damascus: Al-Yamâma, 1992.

al-Dhahabî, Muḥammad ibn Aḥmad. *Kitâb al-Mushtabih fî al-Rijâl: Asmâ'ihim wa Ansâbihim*. 2 vols. Beirut, 1962.

Encyclopaedia of Islam. 1st ed. 9 vols. Leiden: E. J. Brill, 1913–1936.

Encyclopaedia of Islam. New Edition. 8 vols. to date. Leiden: E. J. Brill, 1954–.

al-Faryâbî, Abû Bakr Jaᶜfar ibn Muḥammad ibn al-Ḥasan. *Kitâb Faḍâ'il al-Qur'ân wa Mâ Jâ'a fîhi min al-Faḍl wa fî Kam Yuqra' wa al-Sunna fî Dhâlik*. Edited by Yûsuf ᶜUthmân Faḍl Allâh Jibrîl. Riyâḍ: Maktabat al-Rushd, 1989.

al-Fayrûzabâdî, Majduddîn Muḥammad ibn Yaᶜqûb. *Baṣâ'ir Dhawî al-Tamyîz fî Laṭâ'if al-Kitâb al-ᶜAzîz*. Edited by Muḥammad ᶜAlî al-Najjâr. 8 vols. Beirut: Maktaba al-ᶜIlmiyya, n.d.

al-Funaysân, Saᶜûd ibn ᶜAbdullâh. *Marwiyyât Umm al-Mu'minîn ᶜÂ'isha fî al-Tafsîr*. 3 vols. Riyâḍ: Maktabat Al-Tawba, 1992.

al-Ghazâlî, Abû Ḥâmid Muḥammad al-Ṭûsî. *Jawâhir al-*

Qur'ân. Edited by Muḥammad Rashîd Riḍa al-Qabbânî. Beirut: Dâr Iḥyâ' ᶜUlûm, 1985.

______. *Al-Mustaṣfâ min ᶜIlm al-Uṣûl*. 2 vols. Bulâq, Egypt: Amîriyya Press, 1322–24/1905–7.

______. *The Ninety-Nine Beautiful Names of God*. Translated by David B. Burrell and Nazih Daher. Cambridge: Islamic Texts Society, 1992.

al-Ghazâlî, Muḥammad. *Kayfa Nataᶜâmal maᶜ al-Qur'ân*. Compiled by ᶜUmar ᶜUbayd Ḥasana. Herndon, Va.: Al-Maᶜhad al-ᶜÂlamî li al-Fikr al-Islâmî, 1991.

al-Ḥâkim, Muḥammad ibn ᶜAbdullâh al-Nîsâbûrî. *Al-Mustadrak*. 4 vols. Hyderabad: n.p., 1334/1915.

al-Hamadhânî, Ḥusayn ibn Abî al-ᶜIzz. *Al-Farîd fî Iᶜrâb al-Qur'ân al-Majîd*. Edited by Fahmi Ḥasan al-Nimr and Fu'âd ᶜAlî Mukhaymar. 4 vols. Al-Dûḥa, Qatar: Dâr al-Thaqâfa, 1411/1991.

Hammad, Ahmad Zaki. *Islamic Law: Understanding Juristic Differences*. Indianapolis: American Trust Publications, 1992.

______. *Lasting Prayers of the Quran and the Prophet Muḥammad* ﷺ. Oak Lawn, IL: Quranic Literacy Institute, 1996.

Ḥawwa, Saᶜîd. *Al-Asâs al-Tafsîr*. Cairo: Dâr al-Salâm, 1985.

al-Ḥimayrî, ᶜAbd al-Munᶜim. *Kitâb al-Rawḍ al-Miᶜṭâr fî Khabar al-Aqṭâr*. Edited by Iḥsân ᶜAbbâs. Beirut: Library of Lebanon, 1975.

al-Hindî, ᶜAlâ'uddîn ᶜAlî al-Muttaqqî ibn Ḥusâmuddîn. *Kanz al-ᶜUmmâl fî Sunan al-Aqwâl wa al-Afᶜâl*. 15 vols. Beirut: Mu'assasat al-Risâla, 1979.

al-Ḥumûd, Muḥammad ibn Ḥamad. *Al-Nahj al-Asmâ' fî Sharḥ Asmâ' Allâh al-Ḥusnâ*. 2 vols. Kuwait: Maktabat al-Imâm al-Dhahabî, 1413/1992.

Ibn al-ʿArabî, Abû Bakr Muḥammad ibn ʿAbdullâh. *Aḥkâm al-Qur'ân*. Edited by ʿAlî Muḥammad al-Bijâwî. 2 vols. Beirut: Dâr al-Fikr, n.d.

______. *Qânûn al-Ta'wîl*. Edited by Muḥammad al-Sulaymânî. Beirut: Mu'assasat ʿUlûm al-Qur'ân, 1406/1986.

Ibn Ḥajar al-ʿAsqalânî, Aḥmad. *Fatḥ al-Bârî bi Sharḥ Ṣaḥîḥ al-Bukhârî*. 13 vols. Riyâḍ: Maktabat al-Riyâḍ al-Ḥadîtha, n.d.

______. *Ghirâs al-Asâs*. Edited by Tawfîq Shâhîn. Cairo: Makatabat Wahba, 1990.

______. *Tabṣîr al-Muntabih bi Taḥrîr al-Mushtabih*. Edited by ʿAlî Muḥammad al-Bijâwî. Cairo: The Egyptian Organization for Authorship and Translation, 1965.

Ibn Ḥanbal, Aḥmad. *Marwiyyât al-Imâm Aḥmad Ibn Ḥanbal fî al-Tafsîr*. Compiled and edited by Aḥmad Aḥmad al-Bazra, Muḥammad ibn Rizq ibn al-Ṭarhûnî, and Ḥikmat Bashîr Yâsîn. 4 vols. Riyaḍ: Maktabat al-Mu'ayyad, 1994.

Ibn Hisham, Abû Muḥammad ʿAbd al-Malik. *Al-Sîra al-Nabawî li Ibn Hishâm*. 4 vols. Edited by Muṣṭafâ al-Saqâ, Ibrâhîm al-Ibyârî, and ʿAbd al-Ḥafîẓ Shalabî. Beirut: Dâr al-Qalam, n.d.

______. *Musnad*. 6 vols. Beirut: Al-Maktab al-Islâmî, 1969.

Ibn al-Humâm, Kamâluddîn Muḥammad. *Sharḥ Fatḥ al-Qadîr*. Beirut: Dâr Ṣâdir, n.d.

Ibn al-Jawzî, Jamâluddîn Abû al-Faraj ʿAbd al-Raḥmân ibn ʿAlî. *Funûn al-Afnân fî ʿUyûn ʿUlûm al-Qur'ân*. Edited by Ḥasan Ḍiyâ'uddin ʿItr. Beirut: Dâr al-Bashâ'ir al-Islâmiyya, 1408/1987.

______. *Nawâsikh al-Qur'ân*. Edited by Muḥammad Ashraf ʿAlî al-Malbârî. Madinah: Al-Jâmiʿat al-Islâmiyya bi al-Madînah al-Munawwara. Al-Majlis al-ʿIlmî Iḥyâ' al-Turâth al-Islâmî, 1404/1984.

______. *Nuzhat al-Aʿyun al-Nawâẓir fî ʿIlm al-Wujûh wa al-Naẓâ'ir*. Edited by Sayyida Mehrunnisa. 2 vols. Hyderabad: Maṭbûʿât Dâ'ira al-Maʿârif ʿUthmâniyya (Osmania Oriental Publications Bureau), 1974.

______. *Tadhkirat al-Arîb fî Tafsîr al-Gharîb*. Edited by ʿAlî Ḥusayn al-Bawwâb. 2 vols. Riyâḍ: Maktabat al-Maʿârif, 1986.

______. *Zâd al-Masîr fî ʿIlm al-Tafsîr*. 9 vols. Damascus: Al-Maktab al-Islâmî, 1384/1964.

Ibn Juzayy, Muḥammad ibn Aḥmad al-Kalbî. *Kitâb al-Tashîl li ʿUlûm al-Tanzîl*. 4 parts in 1 vol. Beirut: Dâr al-Kitâb al-ʿArabî, n.d.

Ibn Kathîr, Imâduddîn Abû al-Fidâ' Ismâʿîl. *Al-Mukhtaṣar Tafsîr Ibn Kathîr*. Edited by Muḥammad ʿAlî al-Ṣâbûnî. 3 vols. Beirut: Dâr al-Qur'ân al-Karîm, n.d.

______. *Tafsîr al-Qur'ân al-ʿAẓîm*, 4 vols. Beirut: Dâr al-Fikr. n.d.

Ibn Khâlawayh, Abû ʿAbdullâh al-Ḥusayn ibn Aḥmad. *Kitâb Iʿrâb Thalâthîn Sûra min al-Qur'ân al-Karîm*. Cairo: Maktabat al-Mutanabbî, n.d.

Ibn Manẓûr, Abû al-Faḍl Jamâluddîn ibn Mukarram. *Lisân al-ʿArab*. 15 vols. Cairo: Dâr Ṣâdir, n.d.

Ibn al-Qayyim, Shams al-Dîn Muḥammad ibn Abû Bakr ibn Ayyûb ibn Saʿad ibn Ḥarîz al-Zuraʿî ibn Qayyim al-Jawziyya. *Al-Tafsîr al-Qayyim li al-Imâm Ibn al-Qayyim*. Compiled by Muḥammad Uways al-Nadwî. Edited by Muḥammad Ḥâmid al-Fiqî. Beirut: Dâr al-Fikr, 1408/1988.

Ibn Qutayba al-Dînawarî, Abû Muḥammad. *Ta'wîl Mushkil al-Qur'ân*. Edited by Sayyid Aḥmad Ṣaqr. 3d ed. Madinah: Al-Makatabat al-ʿIlmiyya, 1981.

Ibn Rushd, Abû al-Walîd. *Bidâyat al-Mujtahid wa Nihâyat al-Muqtaṣid*. 2 vols. Beirut: Dâr al-Fikr, n.d.

Ibn Sîdah, Abû al-Ḥasan ᶜAlî ibn Ismâᶜîl al-Naḥwî. *Al-Mukhaṣṣaṣ*. 17 parts in 5 vols. Beirut: Dâr al-Kutub al-ᶜIlmiyya, n.d.

Ibn Ṭarhûnî, Muḥammad ibn Rizq. *Mawsûᶜat Faḍâ'il Suwar wa Âyât al-Qur'ân*. 2 vols. Dammâm: Dâr Ibn al-Qayyim, 1409/1988.

Ibn Taymiyya, Aḥmad ibn ᶜAbd al-Ḥalîm. *Daqâ'iq al-Tafsîr*. Edited by Muḥammad al-Sayyid. 3d ed. 6 vols. in 3. Beirut: Mu'assasat ᶜUlûm al-Qur'ân, 1406/1986.

______. *Majmûᶜ al-Fatâwâ*. 39 vols. Rabat: Maktabat al-Maᶜârif, n.d.

Ibn ᶜUyayna, Sufyân. *Tafsîr Sufyân Ibn ᶜUyayna*. Compiled and edited by Aḥmad Ṣâliḥ Maḥâyrî. Beirut: Maktab al-Islâmî; Riyâḍ: Maktabat Usâma, 1403/1983.

Ibn al-Zubayr, Abû Jaᶜfar Aḥmad ibn Ibrâhîm al-Andalusî al-Ghurnâṭî. *Milâk al-Ta'wîl: Al-Qâṭiᶜ bi Dhawî al-Ilḥâd wa al-Taᶜṭîl fî Tawjîh al-Mutashâbih al-Lafẓ min Ây al-Tanzîl*. Edited by Maḥmûd Kâmil Aḥmad. Beirut: Dâr al-Nahḍa al-ᶜArabiyya, 1985.

ᶜIlaywî, Ibn Khalîfa. *Jâmiᶜ al-Nuqûl fî Asbâb al-Nuzûl wa Sharḥ Âyâtihâ*. 2 vols. Riyâḍ: Maṭâbiᶜ al-Shuᶜâᶜ, 1984.

ᶜInâyat, Ghâzî. *Asbâb al-Nuzûl al-Qur'ânî*. Beirut: Dâr al-Jîl, 1991.

Izutsu, Toshihiko. *Ethico-Religious Concepts in the Qur'ân*. Montreal: McGill University Press, 1966.

al-Jawharî, Ismâᶜîl ibn Ḥammâd. *Al-Ṣiḥâḥ*. Beirut: Dâr al-Ḥaḍâra al-ᶜArabiyya, 1957.

al-Jazâ'irî, Abû Bakr Jâbir. *Aysar al-Tafâsîr li Kalâm al-ᶜAliyy al-Kabîr*. 3d ed. 5 vols. Jidda: Râsim, 1410/1990.

al-Jazâ'irî, Ṭâhir ibn Muḥammad Ṣâliḥ al-Samᶜûnî al-Dimashqî. *Al-Tibyân li Baᶜḍ al-Mabâḥith al-Mutaᶜalliqah bi al-Qur'ân ᶜalâ Ṭarîq al-Itqân*. 4th ed. Edited by ᶜAbd al-Fattâḥ Abû Ghuddah. Beirut: Dâr al-Bashâ'ir al-Islâmiyya, 1412/1992.

Kaḥḥâla, ᶜUmar Riḍâ. *Muᶜjam al-Mu'allifîn: Tarâjum Muṣannafî al-Kutub al-ᶜArabiyya*. 15 vols. Beirut: Maktabat al-Muthannâ, 1957.

La Beaume, Jules. *Tafṣîl Âyât al-Qur'ân al-Ḥakîm*. Translated by Muḥammad Fu'âd ᶜAbd al-Bâqî. Beirut: Dâr al-Kitâb al-ᶜArabî, n.d.

Lane, Edward William. *An Arabic-English Lexicon*. 8 parts (Parts 6–8 edited by Stanley Lane-Poole). 1872. Reprint. Beirut: Librairie du Liban, 1980.

al-Mahallî, Jalâluddîn. *Tafsîr al-Imâmayn al-Jalâlayn* (from Sûrat al-Kahf to Sûrat al-Nâs by Jalâluddîn al-Mahallî. From Sûrat al-Baqara to Sûrat al-Isrâ' by al-Suyûṭî). Beirut: Dâr al-Fikr, n.d.

Majmaᶜ al-Lughat al-ᶜArabiyya (Academy of Arabic Language, Egypt). *Muᶜjam Alfâẓ al-Qur'ân al-Karîm*. Cairo: Dâr al-Shurûq, 1981.

Mâlik ibn Anas. *Al-Muwaṭṭa'*. Edited by Muḥammad Fu'âd ᶜAbd al-Bâqî. 2 vols. n.p.: Dâr al-Turâth al-ᶜArabî, n.d.

al-Manâwî, Zayn al-Dîn ᶜAbd al-Ra'ûf. *Al-Fatḥ al-Samâwî bi Takhrîj Aḥâdîth Tafsîr al-Qâḍî al-Bayḍâwî*. 3 vols. Edited by Aḥmad Mujtabâ ibn Nadhîr ᶜÂlim al-Salafî. Riyâḍ: Dâr al-ᶜÂṣima, 1409/1989.

al-Mâwardî, Abû al-Ḥasan ᶜAlî ibn Ḥabîb. *Tafsîr al-Mâwardî*. 4 vols. Kuwait: Maqhawî Press, 1402/1982.

Mawdûdî, Sayyid Abû al-Aᶜlâ. *Towards Understanding the Qur'ân* (English Version of *Tafhîm al-Qur'ân*). Translated and edited by Zafar Ishaq Ansari (assisted by A. R.

Kidwai). 3 vols. to date. Leicester, UK: The Islamic Foundation, 1988.

Muḥammad, Muḥammad Muṣṭafâ. *Al-Fihras al-Mawḍûʿî li Âyât al-Qur'ân al-Karîm*. 4th ed. Ammân: Dâr ʿAmmâr; Beirut: Dâr al-Jîl, 1409/1989.

Mûsâ, Ḥasan Muḥammad. *Qâmûs Qur'ânî*. Alexandria: Khalîl Ibrâhîm Press, 1966.

Mûsâ, Ḥusayn Yûsuf, and ʿAbd al-Fattâḥ al-Ṣaʿîdî. *Al-Ifṣâḥ fî Fiqh al-Lugha*. 2 vols. Cairo: Dâr al-Fikr al-ʿArabî, 1964.

Muslim ibn al-Ḥajjâj, al-Qushayrî. *Ṣaḥîḥ Muslim*. Edited by Muḥammad Fu'âd ʿAbd al-Bâqî. Cairo: Dâr Iḥyâ' al-Turâth al-ʿArabî, 1955–56. Reprint (5 vols.). Beirut: Dâr al-Fikr, 1978.

Muṣṭafâ, Ibrâhîm; Ḥâmid ʿAbd al-Qâdir; Ḥasan al-Zayyât; and Muḥammad al-Najjâr. *Al-Muʿjam al-Wasîṭ*. 2 vols. Tehran: al-Maktabat al-ʿIlmiyya, n.d.

al-Nasâ'î, Abû ʿAbd al-Raḥmân Aḥmad ibn Shuʿayb ibn ʿAlî. *Faḍâ'il al-Qur'ân*. Edited by Fârûq Ḥamâda. Beirut: Dâr Iḥyâ' al-ʿUlûm; Al-Dâr al-Bayḍâ' [Casablanca]: Dâr al-Thaqâfa, 1413/1992.

______. *Sunan al-Nasâ'î*. 4 vols. (8 parts). Beirut: Dâr al-Kitâb al-ʿArabî, n.d.

______. *Tafsîr al-Nasâ'î*. Edited by Ṣabrî ibn ʿAbd al-Khâliq al-Shâfiʿî and Sayyid ibn ʿAbbâs al-Jalîmîy. 2 vols. Cairo: Maktabat al-Sunna, 1990.

al-Qâsimî, Muḥammad Jamâluddin. *Tafsîr al-Qur'ân*. 17 vols. in 10. Beirut: Dâr al-Fikr, 1978.

al-Qurṭubî, Abû ʿAbdullâh Muḥammad ibn Aḥmad al-Anṣârî. *Al-Jâmiʿ li Aḥkâm al-Qur'ân*. 20 vols. Cairo: Dâr al-Kutub al-Misriyya, 1952–67.

Quṭb, Muḥammad. *Dirâsât Qur'âniyya*. 3d ed. Beirut (and Cairo): Dâr al-Shurûq, 1402/1982.

Quṭb, Sayyid. *Fî Ẓilâl al-Qur'ân*. 6 vols. Beirut: Dâr al-Shurûq, 1393/1973.

al-Râzî, al-Fakhr. *Al-Tafsîr al-Kabîr*. 3d ed. 32 vols. in 15. Beirut: Dâr Iḥyâ' al-Turâth al-ʿArabî, n.d.

Riḍâ, Muḥammad Rashîd. *Tafsîr al-Qur'an al-Ḥakîm* (known as *Tafsîr al-Manâr*). 2d ed. 12 vols. Beirut: Dâr al-Maʿrifa, n.d.

al-Ṣabbâgh, Muḥammad ibn Luṭfî. *Buḥûth fî Uṣûl al-Tafsîr*. Beirut: Al-Maktab al-Islâmî, 1408/1988.

al-Ṣâbûnî, Muḥammad ʿAlî, ed. *Ṣafwat al-Tafâsîr*. 4th ed. 3 vols. Beirut: Dâr al-Qur'ân al-Karîm, 1402/1981.

Ṣâliḥ, Muḥammad Adîb. *Tafsîr al-Nuṣûṣ fî al-Fiqh al-Islâmî*. 2 vols. Beirut: Al-Maktab al-Islâmî, n.d.

al-Sayyid, ʿAbd al-Ḥamîd Muṣṭafâ. *Al-Afʿâl fî al-Qur'ân al-Karîm*. 3 vols. Jeddah: Dâr Bayân al-ʿArabî, 1986.

Shâhîn, ʿAbd al-Ṣabûr. *Mafṣal Ayât al-Qur'ân*. 10 vols. Cairo: n.p., 1989.

Shaltût, Maḥmûd. *Tafsîr al-Qur'ân al-Karîm*. 6th ed. Beirut: Dâr al-Shurûq, 1394/1974.

al-Shawkânî, Muḥammad ibn ʿAlî ibn Muḥammad. *Fatḥal-Qadîr*. 5 vols. Beirut: Dâr Iḥyâ' al-Turâth al-ʿArabî, n.d.

______. *Nayl al-Awṭâr*. 9 vols. Beirut: Dâr al-Jîl, 1973.

Shorter Encyclopaedia of Islam. Edited by H. A. R. Gibb and J. H. Kramers. Leiden: E. J. Brill, 1953.

al-Suddî al-Kabîr, Abû Muḥammad Ismâʿîl ibn ʿAbd al-Raḥmân. *Tafsîr al-Suddî al-Kabîr*. Compiled by Muḥammad ʿAṭâ Yûsuf. Manṣûra: Dâr al-Wafâ', 1993.

al-Suyûṭî, ʿAbd al-Raḥmân ibn al-Kamâl Jamâluddin. *Al-Itqân fî ʿUlûm al-Qur'ân*. Edited by Muḥammad Abû al-Faḍl Ibrâhîm. 3d ed. Cairo: Dâr al-Turâth, 1985.

______. *Lubâb al-Nuqûl fî Asbâb al-Nuzûl*. Beirut: Dâr Iḥyâ' al-ʿUlûm, 1978.

______. *Tafsîr al-Durr al-Manthûr fî al-Tafsîr al-Ma'thûr*. 8 vols. Beirut: Dâr al-Fikr, 1403/1983.

______. *Tafsîr al-Imâmayn al-Jalâlayn* (from Sûrat al-Kahf to Sûrat al-Nâs by Jalâluddîn al-Maḥallî. From Sûrat al-Baqara to Sûrat al-Isrâ' by al-Suyûṭî). Beirut: Dâr al-Fikr, n.d.

al-Ṭabarî, Abû Jaʿfar Muḥammad ibn Jarîr. *Ikhtilâf al-Fuqahâ'*. 2d ed. Beirut, 1902.

______. *Jâmiʿ al-Bayân ʿan Ta'wîl [ây] al-Qur'ân*. 3d ed. 30 vols. in 12. Cairo: Al-Ḥalabî Press, 1968.

______. *Jâmiʿ al-Bayân fî Tafsîr al-Qur'ân*. 12 vols. Beirut: Dâr al-Kutub al-ʿIlmiyya, 1412/1992.

______. *Mukhtaṣar Tafsîr al-Ṭabarî*. Edited by Muḥammad ʿAlî al-Ṣâbûnî and Ṣâliḥ Aḥmad Riḍâ. 2 vols. Beirut: Dâr al-Qur'ân al-Karîm, 1403/1983.

al-Thawrî, ibn ʿAbdullâh Sufyân ibn Saʿîd. *Tafsîr Sufyân al-Thawrî*. Beirut: Dâr al-Kutb al-ʿIlmiyya, 1403/1983.

al-Tirmidhî, Muḥammad ibn ʿÎsâ. *Sunan al-Tirmidhî*. 10 vols. Cairo: Al-Ḥalabî Press, 1965–68.

U. A. E. Ministry. *Al-Muntakhab fî Tafsîr al-Qur'ân al-Karîm*. United Arab Emirates, n.d.

al-ʿUkbarî, Abû al-Baqâ' ʿAbdullâh ibn al-Ḥusayn. *Al-Mashûf al-Muʿlim fî Tartîb al-Iṣlâḥ ʿAla Ḥurûf al-Muʿjam*. Edited by Yâsîn Muḥammad al-Sawwâs. 2 vols. Makkah: Al-Jâmiʿat Umm al-Qura, n.d.

al-Wâdiʿî, Abû ʿAbd al-Raḥmân Muqbil ibn Hâdî. *Al-Ṣaḥîḥ al-Musnad min Asbâb al-Nuzûl*. 4th ed. Cairo: Maktabat Ibn Taymiyya, 1408/1987.

Wensinck, A. J. *Concordance et Indices de la Traditione Musulmane.* 7 vols. Leiden: E. J. Brill, 1936–1969.

al-Zabîdî, Muḥammad Murtaḍa al-Ḥusaynî. *Tâj al-ʿArûs min Jawâhir al-Qamûs.* 10 vols. Cairo: Khayriyya Press, 1306/1888.

al-Ẓâhirî, Abû Turâb. *Shawâhid al-Qur'ân.* 2 vols. Jeddah: Literary Cultural Club, 1989.

al-Zajjâjî, Abû al-Qâsim ʿAbd al-Raḥmân ibn Isḥâq. *Ishtiqâq Asmâ' Allâh.* 2d ed. Beirut: Mu'assasat al-Risâla, 1986.

al-Zamakhsharî, Muḥammad ibn ʿUmar. *Al-Kashshâf ʿan Ḥaqâ'iq al-Tanzîl wa ʿUyûn al-Aqâwîl fî Wujûh al-Ta'wîl.* 4 vols. Beirut: Dâr al-Maʿrifa, n.d.

al-Zarkashî, Badruddîn. *Al-Burhân fî ʿUlûm al-Qur'ân.* 3d ed. Edited by Muḥammad Abû Faḍl Ibrâhîm. 4 vols. n.p.: Dâr al-Fikr, 1980.

al-Zâwî, al-Ṭâhir Aḥmad. *Tartîb al-Qâmûs.* 2d ed. 4 vols. Beirut: Dâr al-Fikr, n.d.

Zaylaʿî, Jamâluddîn Abû Muḥammad ʿAbdullâh ibn Yûsuf al-Ḥanafî. *Nasb al-Râyyah li Aḥâdîth al-Hidâya.* 2d ed. 4 vols. n.p.: Al-Maktaba al-Islâmiyya, 1973.

al-Zayn, Samîḥ ʿÂṭif. *Al-Iʿrâb fî al-Qur'ân al-Karîm.* Beirut: Dâr al-Kitâb al-Lubnânî, 1405/1985.

al-Zuḥaylî, Wahba. *Al-Fiqh al-Islâmî wa Adillatuh.* 2d ed. 8 vols. Damascus: Dâr al-Fikr, 1985.

______. *Al-Tafsîr al-Munîr fî al-ʿAqîda wa al-Sharîʿa wa al-Manhaj.* 32 parts in 16 vols. Beirut: Dâr al-Fikr al-Muʿâṣir; Damascus: Dâr al-Fikr, 1411/1991.

8

ḤADÎTH INDEX

PROPHET MUḤAMMAD ﷺ related:

Allah, the Almighty and the Majestic, has said, "I have apportioned the Prayer (al-Fâtiḥa) between Myself and My worshipper in two parts—and My worshipper shall have what he has asked for."

So when the worshipper says, "*All Praise is for Allah, Lord of the Worlds,*" Allah says, "My worshipper has praised Me."

When he says, "*The All-Merciful, the Mercy-Giving,*" Allah says, "My worshipper has extolled Me."

When he says, "*Master of the Day of Judgment,*" Allah says, "My worshipper has magnified Me and entrusted Me with his affairs."

When he says, "*It is You we worship, and it is You we ask for help,*" Allah says, "This is between Myself and My worshipper—and My worshipper shall have what he has asked for."

When he says, "*Guide us to the straight way, the way of those upon whom You have bestowed grace, not those upon whom there is wrath, nor those astray,*" Allah says, "This is for My worshipper—and My worshipper shall have what he has asked for."

PAGES: 7–8
SOURCE: *Ṣaḥîḥ Muslim,* 1:296.

AT THE VERY beginning of his mission, the Prophet ﷺ confided in his wife Khadijah, "When I am all alone, I hear a call, and, by God, I fear for myself!" She suggested that he consult her learned cousin, Waraqa ibn Nawfal, a Makkan scriptural sage, who advised the Prophet not to turn away from the call nor to fear it.

PAGE: 9
SOURCE: Al-Suyûṭî, *al-Itqân fî ʿUlûm al-Qur'ân*, 1:70–71; and *Ṣaḥîḥ al-Bukhârî*, 1:23.

THE PROPHET ﷺ described al-Fâtiḥa, together with the closing verses of Sûrat al-Baqara (2:285–86), as the "two lights [of revelation] without equal in the Torah, the Psalms, or the Gospel."

PAGE: 9
SOURCE: *Sunan al-Nasâ'î*, 2:138.

"THE GREATEST CHAPTER of the Quran" is how the Prophet of Islam ﷺ described al-Fâtiḥa.

PAGE: 10
SOURCE: *Ṣaḥîḥ al-Bukhârî*, 9:54.

THE PROPHET ﷺ SAID, "Any significant act that does not begin 'in the name of Allah' is severed," that is, cut off from reward or benefit.

PAGES: 13, 38
SOURCE: Ibn Kathîr, *Tafsîr al-Qur'ân al-ʿAẓîm*, 1:18; and al-Hindî, *Kanz al-ʿUmmâl fî Sunan al-Aqwâl wa al-Afʿâl*, 1:555, 558.

"WHOEVER DOES NOT thank people does not thank Allah," said the Prophet of Islam ﷺ, revealing the wider connection of relations among human beings as based on their relationship with God.

PAGE: 15
SOURCE: *Musnad Aḥmad*, 2:258

THE PROPHET ﷺ OFTEN said during the night:

O Allah, for You is all praise! You are the light of the heavens and the earth. For You is all praise! You are the Sustainer of the heavens and the earth. For You is all praise! You are the Lord of the heavens and the earth and all therein. You are the Truth. Your promise is the truth. Your word is the truth. The meeting with You is true. The Garden is true. The Fire is true. The Hour is true.

O Allah, to You I submit. In You I believe. On You I rely. To You I repent. For You I oppose. To You I refer in judgment. So forgive me whatever I may have done and whatever I may do, whatever I have concealed and whatever I have revealed. You are my God. There is no God but You.

PAGE: 15
SOURCE: *Ṣaḥîḥ Muslim,* 1:532–33.

THE PROPHET ﷺ SAID, "Allah has a hundred mercies. It is through one of these mercies that all creatures show mercy to one another, while ninety-nine mercies remain [with Him] for the Day of Resurrection."

PAGE: 16
SOURCE: *Ṣaḥîḥ Muslim,* 4:2108.

THE PROPHET ﷺ SAID that God has stated:

O son of Adam, I have sent to you seven [verses]: Three for Me, three for you, and one between you and Myself.

As for the three of Mine, they are: *In the name of Allah, the All-Merciful, the Mercy-Giving*; *All Praise is for Allah, Lord of the Worlds*; and *the All-Merciful, the Mercy-Giving.*

As for the three for you, they are: *Master of the Day of Judgment*; *Guide us to the straight way*; and *the way of those upon whom You have bestowed grace, not those upon whom there is wrath, nor those astray.*

The one between us is, *It is You we worship, and it is You we ask for help* (meaning *worship* from the worshipper and *help* from Allah, the Exalted).

PAGES: 18–19
SOURCE: Ibn al-ʿArabî, *Aḥkâm al-Qur'ân*, 1:5.

THE PROPHET ﷺ PRAYED:

O Allah, You are my Lord. There is no God but You. You created me, and I am Your servant. I uphold Your covenant and promise, as much as I am able. I seek refuge in You from the harm of whatever I may have done. To You I acknowledge Your grace upon me, and to You I bring my sins. Forgive me, for truly no one forgives sins except You.

PAGES: 19–20
SOURCE: *Ṣaḥîḥ al-Bukhârî*, 11:97–98.

THE PROPHET ﷺ RELATED that God has said:

O My servants, all of you are astray but those whom I guide; so seek guidance of Me, and I shall guide you. O My servants, all of you are hungry but those I feed; so seek food of Me, and I shall feed you. O My servants, all of you are naked but those I clothe; so seek clothing of Me, and I shall clothe you. O My servants, you err by night and by day, and I forgive all sins; so seek forgiveness of Me, and I shall forgive you.

PAGE: 20
SOURCE: *Ṣaḥîḥ Muslim*, 4:1994–95.

AFTER LEARNING OF three youthful Companions who had taken vows to pray all night without rest, fast every day without break, and remain celibate, the Prophet of Islam ﷺ said, "I pray in the night and I sleep; I fast and I break my fast; and I marry women."

PAGE: 21
SOURCE: *Ṣaḥîḥ Muslim*, 2:1020.

THE PROPHET ﷺ OFTEN prayed:

O Allah, I am indeed Your servant, the son of Your servant, the son of Your maidservant. My forelock is in Your hand. Your decree upon me is done, and Your judgment upon me is just. I beseech You by every one of Your names—with which You have named Yourself, or have taught to any one among Your creation, or have sent down in Your Book, or have kept to Yourself in the knowledge of the unseen—to make the Quran the springtime of my heart, the light within my chest, the departure of my sadness, and the vanishing of my worries.

PAGE: 22
SOURCE: *Musnad Aḥmad,* 1:391.

THE PROPHET ﷺ EXHORTED his companions to appeal for God's help after each prayer by saying, "O Allah, help me to remember You always and be thankful to You, and to worship You in the most excellent way."

PAGE: 22
SOURCE: *Sunan al-Nasâ'î,* 3:53.

A STATEMENT OF the Prophet ﷺ illustrates the significance of adhering to the straight way and overcoming the temptations:

Allah has given the likeness of a straight way. On both sides of this way are two walls with open doors. On the doors are hanging drapes. At the gateway is a caller who says, "O people, enter the way all together, and do not turn off from it," along with another caller calling from [deep] within the way. When a person desires to open any of these doors, the [latter] caller says, "Woe to you! Do not open it, for if you open it, you will enter it." The way is Islam. The walls are the limits Allah has set. The open doors are the prohibitions of Allah. The caller at the head of the way is the Book of Allah. The caller within the gateway is the warner of Allah in the heart of every Muslim.

PAGE: 23
SOURCE: *Musnad Aḥmad,* 4:183.

AFTER HIS MIGRATION to Madinah, the Prophet ﷺ explained that the verse *those upon whom there is wrath* refers to the Children of Israel who deliberately and repeatedly violated their covenant with God and abandoned the laws of Moses, and that the words *those astray* make reference to Christians who have forsaken the teachings of Jesus and ascribed to God and His prophets what He did not authorize. This concluding appeal—not to be like *those upon whom there is wrath, nor those astray*—

refers to any people who abandon, reject, or manipulate revealed truth.

PAGE: 26
SOURCE: *Musnad Aḥmad,* 4:378–79.

THE PROPHET ﷺ SAID in his Farewell Address: "Let whoever is present convey [the message] to whoever is absent, for [the latter] may comprehend better than one who first heard it."

PAGE: 27
SOURCE: *Ṣaḥîḥ al-Bukhârî,* 1:158.

THE PROPHET ﷺ OFTEN prayed:

In the name of Allah, I rely on Allah. I seek refuge in You from straying or being led astray, from erring or slipping into error, from oppressing or being oppressed, from ignorance or from the ignorance of others against me.

PAGE: 28
SOURCE: *Sunan Abû Dâwûd,* 4:325.

IN RECOGNITION OF al-Fâtiḥa's importance in Islamic worship and Muslim life, the Prophet ﷺ said, "There is no prayer for those who do not recite the Opening of the Book."

PAGE: 29
SOURCE: *Ṣaḥîḥ Muslim,* 1:295.

THE PROPHET ﷺ SAID to his Companions: "When the imam (the leader of the prayer) says, *Not those upon whom there is wrath, nor those astray,* then say, *'Âmîn.'* Whoever's utterance coincides with that of the angels, shall have their sins forgiven."

PAGE: 30
SOURCE: *Ṣaḥîḥ Muslim,* 1:307.

THE PROPHET OF Islam ﷺ said *"Âmîn"* in an audible voice, as did those who prayed with him, in the vocalized portions of the Dawn, Sunset, and Evening Prayers.

PAGE: 30
SOURCE: *Ṣaḥîḥ Muslim,* 1:307.

ABÛ SAʿÎD IBN al-Muʿalla, narrated:

Once I was praying in the mosque and the Prophet ﷺ called me, but I did not respond to him [until finishing the Prayer]. "O Messenger of God," I later said, "I was praying."

[The Prophet ﷺ] then said, "Did Allah not say, *'Respond to Allah and to the Messenger when he calls you. . . .'*?" (8:24)

Then he said to me, "Shall I not teach you the greatest sura of the Quran before you leave the mosque?" And he took my hand.

So when we wanted to leave, I said, "O Messenger of Allah, you said, 'I shall teach you the greatest sura of the Quran.'"

He said, *"All praise is for Allah, Lord of the Worlds.* It is the Seven Oft-Repeated [Verses] and the magnificent Quran that has been given to me."

PAGES: 30–31
SOURCE: *Ṣaḥîḥ al-Bukhârî,* 9:54.

ACCORDING TO THE Companion Abû Saʿîd al-Khudry, some Companions of the Prophet were traveling when a young girl came running to them and said, "The chief of this area has been stung and our men are away. Are any of you healers?" So one of the Companions, whom the others had never known to be associated with healing, went with her. He then recited something over the chief, who thereafter recovered and rewarded him with thirty goats and milk to drink. When he returned, the others said to him, "Have you ever before healed in this manner?" "No," he said. "I only recited [over him] the Mother of the Book (al-Fâtiḥa)." When they returned to the Prophet ﷺ and related the story to him, he approved of this action.

PAGE: 31
SOURCE: *Ṣaḥîḥ al-Bukhârî,* 9:54.

THE PROPHET ﷺ RECITED verses from al-Fâtiḥa when asking God for rain during times of drought.

All praise is for Allah, Lord of the Worlds, the All-Merciful, the Mercy-Giving, Master of the Day of Judgment. There is no God but Allah. He does what He wills. O Allah, You are the only

God, there is no God but You, the Self-Sufficient. And truly we are in need, so bring down to us rainfall. And let what You have brought down for us be a [source of] strength and means for a time.

PAGES: 31–32
SOURCE: *Sunan Abû Dâwûd,* 1:304.

IN ACKNOWLEDGING THE importance of kinship and the role of motherhood, the Prophet ﷺ said that in describing His designation of the womb as *raḥim,* Allah has stated, "I am *al-Raḥmân* (the All-Merciful) and have created the *raḥim* (the womb) and derived its name from Mine. So whoever brings it close, I will bring close; and whoever severs it, I will sever."

PAGE: 39
SOURCE: *Musnad Aḥmad,* 1:191.

THE PROPHET ﷺ SAID that might is not knocking down one's opponent, but in restraining oneself when angry.

PAGE: 65
SOURCE: *Ṣaḥîḥ Muslim,* 4:2014.

THE PROPHET ﷺ SAID, "There is no ablution for whoever does not mention the name of Allah before it."

PAGE: 72–73 (Note 9)
SOURCE: *Sunan al-Tirmidhî,* 1:37–39, #25, 26.

IN SEEKING REFUGE against harm, the Prophet ﷺ would say three times, "In the name of Allah, with whose name nothing can be harmed in the earth nor in the heavens. He is the All-Hearing, the All-Knowing."

PAGE: 73 (Note 9)
SOURCE: *Sunan al-Tirmidhî,* 5:434, #3388.

BEFORE SLEEPING, THE Prophet ﷺ would say, "In the name of Allah, I lay my side down. O Allah, forgive me my sins and impel away my devil and release my debts and place me among the highest assembly."

PAGE: 73 (Note 9)
SOURCE: *Sunan Abû Dâwûd,* 4:313, #5054.

9

QURANIC VERSE INDEX

Al-Fâtiḥa: Sura 1

1:1 .... *pp.* 5, 12, 38
1:2 .... *pp.* 5–7, 11, 14, 19, 31, 42, 44
1:3 .... *pp.* 5–7, 16, 19, 31, 34, 41
1:4 .... *pp.* 5–7, 16–17, 19, 23, 31, 47, 50
1:5 .... *pp.* 5–6, 8, 18–19, 24, 54, 61
1:6 .... *pp.* 5, 7–8, 19, 23–24, 55, 61
1:7 .... *pp.* 5, 8, 19, 25

Al-Baqara: Sura 2

2:2 .... *pp.* 55, 58
2:8 .... *p.* 49
2:20 .... *p.* 60
2:31 .... *p.* 35
2:45 .... *pp.* 42, 54
2:62 .... *p.* 49
2:68 .... *p.* 53
2:85 .... *p.* 49
2:90 .... *p.* 65
2:107 .... *p.* 46
2:137 .... *p.* 56
2:142, 213 ...... *p.* 56
2:153 .... *p.* 54
2:185 .... *p.* 21
2:196 .... *p.* 57
2:201 .... *p.* 21
2:229 .... *p.* 60
2:231 .... *p.* 64
2:246–47 .... *p.* 47
2:255 .... *p.* 61
2:267 .... *p.* 42
2:282 .... *pp.* 36, 51
2:285–86 .... *p.* 9

Âl ʿImrân: Sura 3

3:8 .... *p.* 56
3:9, 25 .... *p.* 49
3:26 .... *p.* 46
3:36 .... *p.* 35
3:83 .... *p.* 50
3:85 .... *p.* 50
3:101 .... *p.* 61
3:112 .... *p.* 65
3:144 .... *p.* 42
3:146 .... *p.* 44
3:188 .... *p.* 42
3:189 .... *p.* 46

Al-Nisâ': Sura 4

4:11–12 .... *p.* 51
4:69 .... *p.* 25
4:93 .... *p.* 64
4:127 .... *p.* 60

4:142 . . . . *p.* 60
4:176 . . . . *p.* 68

Al-Mâ'ida: Sura 5
5:2 . . . . *p.* 54
5:3 . . . . *pp.* 50, 64
5:6 . . . . *p.* 60
5:7 . . . . *p.* 63
5:20 . . . . *p.* 63
5:23 . . . . *p.* 63
5:44, 63 . . . . *p.* 44
5:68 . . . . *p.* 60
5:76 . . . . *p.* 46
5:78 . . . . *p.* 52
5:97 . . . . *p.* 57

Al-Anᶜâm: Sura 6
6:1 . . . . *p.* 42
6:45 . . . . *p.* 42
6:73 . . . . *p.* 47
6:74 . . . . *p.* 67
6:90 . . . . *p.* 56
6:118, 119 . . . . . . *p.* 38
6:126 . . . . *p.* 57
6:153 . . . . *pp.* 57–58

Al-Aᶜrâf: Sura 7
7:16 . . . . *p.* 61
7:43 . . . . *p.* 42
7:52 . . . . *p.* 40
7:60 . . . . *p.* 67
7:86 . . . . *p.* 57
7:128 . . . . *p.* 54
7:150, 154 . . . . . . *p.* 65
7:156 . . . . *p.* 40

Al-Anfâl: Sura 8
8:16 . . . . *p.* 65
8:24 . . . . *p.* 30
8:53 . . . . *p.* 63

Al-Tawba: Sura 9
9:7 . . . . *p.* 59
9:29, 33 . . . . *p.* 50
9:36 . . . . *p.* 50
9:84 . . . . *p.* 59
9:108 . . . . *p.* 59
9:112 . . . . *p.* 42
9:128 . . . . *p.* 41
9:129 . . . . *p.* 43

Yûnus: Sura 10
10:10 . . . . *p.* 14
10:12 . . . . *p.* 59
10:15 . . . . *p.* 49
10:31 . . . . *p.* 46

Hûd: Sura 11
11:17 . . . . *p.* 40
11:41 . . . . *p.* 38

Yûsuf: Sura 12
12:18 . . . . *p.* 54
12:39 . . . . *p.* 44
12:40 . . . . *pp.* 35, 50
12:41, 42, 50 . . . *p.* 44
12:43 . . . . *p.* 47
12:95 . . . . *p.* 68
12:101 . . . . *p.* 46

Ibrâhîm: Sura 14
14:34 . . . . *p.* 63
14:36 . . . . *p.* 68
14:41 . . . . *p.* 60

Al-Ḥijr: Sura 15
15:36 . . . . *p.* 49
15:38 . . . . *p.* 49
15:42 . . . . *p.* 53
15:99 . . . . *p.* 52

Al-Naḥl: Sura 16
16:18 . . . . *p.* 63
16:36 . . . . *p.* 52
16:53 . . . . *p.* 62
16:73 . . . . *p.* 46
16:80 . . . . *p.* 60

16:93 . . . . *p.* 68
16:106 . . . . *p.* 64
16:114 . . . . *p.* 63
16:122 . . . . *p.* 58

Al-Isrâ': Sura 17
17:44 . . . . *p.* 42
17:79 . . . . *p.* 43
17:83 . . . . *p.* 63
17:100 . . . . *p.* 46
17:110 . . . . *p.* 40
17:111 . . . . *pp.* 14, 42

Al-Kahf: Sura 18
18:1 . . . . *p.* 42
18:17 . . . . *p.* 68
18:95 . . . . *p.* 54
18:104 . . . . *p.* 68

Maryam: Sura 19
19:21 . . . . *p.* 40
19:36 . . . . *p.* 58
19:39 . . . . *p.* 49
19:42–48 . . . . *p.* 27
19:58 . . . . *pp.* 25, 63
19:65 . . . . *pp.* 35, 52
19:87 . . . . *p.* 46

Ṭâ Hâ: Sura 20
20:8 . . . . *pp.* 12, 35
20:50 . . . . *p.* 56
20:52 . . . . *p.* 68
20:79 . . . . *p.* 68
20:81 . . . . *p.* 65
20:86 . . . . *p.* 65
20:123 . . . . *p.* 69

Al-Anbiyâ': Sura 21
21:87 . . . . *p.* 65
21:107 . . . . *p.* 40
21:112 . . . . *p.* 54

Al-Ḥajj: Sura 22
22:5 . . . . *p.* 36
22:28, 40 . . . . *p.* 38
22:47 . . . . *p.* 49
22:78 . . . . *p.* 35

Al-Mu'minûn: Sura 23
23:28 . . . . *pp.* 14, 42
23:73 . . . . *p.* 57

Al-Nûr: Sura 24
24:2 . . . . *p.* 50
24:8–9 . . . . *p.* 65
24:56 . . . . *p.* 61

Al-Furqân: Sura 25
25:2 . . . . *p.* 47
25:4 . . . . *p.* 54
25:26 . . . . *p.* 47
25:41–42 . . . . *p.* 67
25:76 . . . . *p.* 60

Al-Shuʿarâ': Sura 26
26:26 . . . . *p.* 43
26:28 . . . . *p.* 43
26:82 . . . . *p.* 50

Al-Naml: Sura 27
27:15 . . . . *p.* 14
27:19 . . . . *p.* 64
27:30 . . . . *p.* 38
27:34 . . . . *p.* 47
27:36 . . . . *p.* 56
27:63 . . . . *p.* 55

Al-Qaṣaṣ: Sura 28
28:77 . . . . *p.* 21

Al-Rûm: Sura 30
30:8 . . . . *p.* 36
30:30 . . . . *p.* 50
30:43 . . . . *p.* 50

Luqmân: Sura 31

31:20 .... *p.* 63
31:29 .... *p.* 36

Al-Sajda: Sura 32

32:4 .... *p.* 49
32:5 .... *p.* 49
32:10 .... *p.* 66

Al-Aḥzâb: Sura 33

33:9 .... *p.* 62
33:13 .... *p.* 60
33:33 .... *p.* 61
33:40 .... *p.* 42
33:43 .... *p.* 41

Sabâ': Sura 34

34:22 .... *p.* 46
34:42 .... *p.* 47

Fâṭir: Sura 35

35:1 .... *p.* 42
35:3 .... *p.* 63
35:8 .... *p.* 68
35:13 .... *p.* 36
35:24 .... *p.* 67
35:34 .... *pp.* 14, 42

Al-Ṣâffât: Sura 37

37:20 .... *p.* 50
37:21 .... *p.* 49
37:23 .... *pp.* 55, 57

Ṣâd: Sura 38

38:16, 26, 53 ... *p.* 49
38:22 .... *p.* 55
38:35 .... *p.* 46

Al-Zumar: Sura 39

39:2, 11, 14 .... *p.* 52
39:3 .... *p.* 50
39:37 .... *p.* 68
39:42 .... *p.* 36

Ghâfir: Sura 40

40:32 .... *p.* 49

Fuṣṣilat: Sura 41

41:6 .... *p.* 59
41:16 .... *p.* 48
41:30 .... *p.* 59
41:51 .... *p.* 63

Al-Shûrâ: Sura 42

42:13 .... *p.* 50
42:37 .... *p.* 65
42:53 .... *p.* 57

Al-Zukhruf: Sura 43

43:27 .... *p.* 56
43:86 .... *p.* 46

Al-Jâthiya: Sura 45

45:36 .... *p.* 42

Al-Aḥqâf: Sura 46

46:3 .... *p.* 36
46:5 .... *p.* 66
46:13–14 .... *p.* 59
46:15 .... *p.* 64

Muḥammad: Sura 47

47:2 .... *p.* 42

Al-Fatḥ: Sura 48

48:25 .... *p.* 57
48:29 .... *pp.* 40, 42

Al-Ḥujurât: Sura 49

49:11 .... *p.* 61

Qâf: Sura 50
50:34 . . . . *p.* 49
50:42 . . . . *p.* 49

Al-Dhâriyât: Sura 51
51:56 . . . . *p.* 52

Al-Najm: Sura 53
53:27 . . . . *p.* 35
53:30 . . . . *p.* 68

Al-Qamar: Sura 54
54:19 . . . . *p.* 48

Al-Wâqiʿa: Sura 56
56:89 . . . . *p.* 63

Al-Mujâdila: Sura 58
58:13 . . . . *p.* 61

Al-Ḥashr: Sura 59
59:24 . . . . *pp.* 35, 39

Al-Mumtaḥina: Sura 60
60:13 . . . . *p.* 64

Al-Ṣaff: Sura 61
61:6 . . . . *p.* 42

Al-Jumuʿa: Sura 62
62:11 . . . . *p.* 59

Al-Taghâbun: Sura 64
64:1 . . . . *p.* 15
64:7 . . . . *p.* 17
64:9 . . . . *p.* 49

Al-Mulk: Sura 67
67:1 . . . . *p.* 47
67:9 . . . . *p.* 68

Al-Qalam: Sura 68
68:2–4 . . . . *p.* 8
68:7 . . . . *p.* 68

Al-Ḥâqqa: Sura 69
69:52 . . . . *p.* 38

Al-Maʿârij: Sura 70
70:4 . . . . *p.* 49
70:26 . . . . *p.* 50

Al-Muzzammil: Sura 73
73:2–4 . . . . *p.* 8

Al-Muddaththir: Sura 74
74:2–7 . . . . *p.* 8
74:31 . . . . *p.* 68
74:46 . . . . *p.* 50

Al-Qiyâma: Sura 75
75:1, 6 . . . . *p.* 61

Al-Insân: Sura 76
76:18 . . . . *p.* 35
76:20 . . . . *p.* 47
76:25 . . . . *p.* 38

Al-Takwîr: Sura 81
81:28 . . . . *p.* 59

Al-Muṭaffifîn: Sura 83
83:11 . . . . *p.* 50
83:32 . . . . *p.* 67

Al-Burûj: Sura 85
85:2 . . . . *p.* 49

Al-Ṭâriq: Sura 86
86:9 . . . . *p.* 49

Al-Aʿlâ: Sura 87
87:3 .... *p.* 56

Al-ʿAlaq: Sura 96
96:1 .... *pp.* 9, 12

Al-Bayyina: Sura 98:
98:4–5 .... *p.* 53
98:5 .... *pp.* 50, 52, 53, 60

Al-Zalzala: Sura 99
99:7–8 .... *p.* 18

Al-Kâfirûn: Sura 109
109:6 .... *p.* 50

Al-Naṣr: Sura 110
110:2 .... *p.* 50
110:3 .... *p.* 42

10

SUBJECT INDEX

Aaron (Prophet Hârûn), a model of grace, 25

ʿAbdu, Muḥammad, 9

Ablution, before Prayer, 60

Abraham (Prophet Ibrâhîm)
- asking for forgiveness, 60
- father of, 26, 58, 67
- guided to the straight way, 57–58
- model of grace, 25
- naming believers, 35
- praising God for granting him children, 14
- uprightness and compassion of, 26
- warning against the worship of Satan, 27

Abû Saʿîd Ibn al-Muʿalla, 30

Abû Saʿîd al-Khudry, 31

Adam (and Eve)
- learning the names, 35
- parents of humanity, 13
- Satan, enemy of, 68

Afterlife (Hereafter)
- benefits of recalling often, 18
- certainty in, 18
- eternal peace of, 21
- Garden and great kingdom in, 47, 63
- names of the Last Day, 48
- Paradise in, 59
- real success in, 12
- *See also* Hell

ʿÂlamîn (عَالَمِين)
- defined, 44–45
- linguistic derivatives of, in Quran: *ʿâlam*, 44–45; *ʿalama*, 44; *ʿalm*, 44; *ʿilm*, 45; *Rabb al-ʿÂlamîn*, 45

Allah (God)
- believers appealing to for guidance, 7, 9, 11
- bestowing grace, 25
- blessedness of, 47
- blessings of, 6, 63
- commandments of, 7, 52, 61, 63
- covenant with, 11, 19, 23, 26, 64, 67
- divine attributes of, 6, 16, 35, 37, 40
- excellent names of, 35, 39, 40
- gives and withdraws authority, 46
- grace of, 62–63
- guidance of, 24, 27, 56, 61, 68
- having no equivalent, 35

Allah (God) (*continued*)
- hears all prayers, 16
- help (assistance) of, 18, 22, 31
- human nature recognizes Him, 11
- inimitable words of, *xii*, *xv*
- invoking and mentioning the name of, 12, 13, 38
- kindness and clemency of, 16
- Lord of all things, 15
- Lordship of, 16, 43
- Love of, 20, 40
- Master of the Day of Judgment, 5–7, 16–17, 19, 23, 31, 47
- mercy of, 16, 39–41, 46, 63
- Muslim reverence for, 14
- names of: *The All-Dominating*, 44; *the All-Forgiving*, 35; *the All-Merciful*, 5–7, 12, 16, 19, 25, 27–28, 31, 34–35, 38–41; *the All-Preserving*, 21; *the All-Trustworthy*, 21; *the Creator*, 6, 12, 14, 17, 67; *the Enricher*, 6; *the Eternal*, 24; *the Everlasting*, 35; *the Faithful*, 7, 12; *the First and the Last*, 12; *the Guardian*, 12, 21; *the Help-Giver*, 19; *the Irresistible*, 12; *Lord of the east and west*, 43; *Lord of the heavens and the earth*, 15, 43; *Lord of the Worlds*, 2, 5–7, 14, 16, 18–19, 31, 42–43, 45; *the Manifest and the Hidden*, 12; *Master of All Domains*, 46; *the Mercy-Giving*, 5–7, 12, 16, 19, 28, 31, 34, 38–41; *the Overpowering*, 12; *the Peace*, 12; *the Proud*, 12; *the Sustainer*, 12, 15, 28
- nurturing and sustaining creation, 6, 16
- originator of creation, 17
- praise of, 15, 42
- recompensing each individual, 48
- reverence for, 14
- reviving all from death, 17
- rewards the good, 17
- right to hear words of, 27
- source of creation, 9, 12
- source of power and vitality, 22
- sovereignty over creation, 46
- teaching Adam the names, 35
- unfailing help of, 6–7
- way of, 8, 57, 66
- willing worship of, 11
- wrath of, 64–65

Allah (الله)
- defined linguistically, 36
- linguistic derivatives of, in Quran: *aliha*, 37; *aliha/ya'lahu*, 37; *Allah*, 37–38; *bismillâh*, 34–36, 38; *ilâh*, 37

Almsgiving (*Zakât*), 22, 61

Âmîn
- implied meaning of, 8
- said after al-Fâtiḥa, 30

Angel of Revelation, 8

Angels
- denial of as disbelief, 66
- extolling God, 42
- given false names by disbelievers, 35
- occurrence in the Quran, 47–48
- rational beings, 45
- saying *Âmîn* with believers, 30
- wrongful worship of by disbelievers, 52

Arabic
- definite article *al*, 37, 56
- idiom of, 1
- linguistic references, 1
- linguists, 36–37
- preposition *bi*, 35–36
- reflexive Arabic particle, 53
- text of al-Fâtiḥa, *xviii*
- and translation, *xvi–xviii*

Aramaic, 37

Ark. *See* Noah (Prophet Nûḥ), Ark of

Astray
  regarding Christians, 26, 67
  See also Ḍâllîn

Basmala (In the name of Allah)
  benefit of invoking, 13
  etiquette of beginnings, 13
  linguistic definition of, 35
  mentioned over food, 38
  Noah embarking the Ark, 38
  universal commencement, 38

Battle of Badr (Day of Badr), 48

Belief
  approach of, 26
  cannot be forced, 26
  choice as a foundation of, 25
  unchanging nature of, 24

Believers and Muslims
  ability to overcome anger, 65
  accused by the wrongdoers of being misguided, 67
  appealing to Allah, 9
  commanded to be straight, 59
  defeating the disbelievers of Quraysh, 48
  establishing Prayer (*Ṣalât*), 61
  mercy among, 40
  non-Arabic speaking, *xviii*, 28
  prohibited to ridicule others, 61
  in quest of moral excellence, 7
  recording loan agreements, 36
  remembering the afterlife, 18
  required to make ablution for Prayer, 60
  thankful to Allah, 14
  upholding justice, 60
  working for the common good, 54

Children of Adam, 17, 25

Children of Israel (or Israelites)
  commanded to seek God's help, 54
  knowledgeable people of, 44
  urging their Prophet to appoint a king, 47
  violating God's commandments, 26
  worshipping golden calf, 65
  wrath of God, 26, 67

Christians
  falsely ascribing to God, 67
  those who forsake the teachings of Jesus, 26
  See also People of the Book

Commentary, definition of, 2

Commentary literature (*tafsîr*), 1

Companion(s) of the Prophet
  Abû Saʿîd Ibn al-Muʿalla, 30
  Abû Saʿîd al-Khudry, 31
  exhorted to seek God's help, 22
  Ibn ʿAbbâs, 14
  Ibn Masʿûd, 30

Creation
  extolling God, 42
  gratitude to, 14–15
  Lord of, 27
  numerousness of, 11
  origin of, 17
  source of, 9, 12
  sovereign of, 46
  sustained and nurtured by God, 6, 16

Ḍâllîn (ضالين)
  defined, 65
  linguistic derivatives of, in Quran: *aḍalla*, 66; *ḍalâl*, 65; *ḍalâl baʿîd*, 66; *ḍalâl kabîr*, 68; *ḍalâl mubîn*, 66; *ḍalâl qadîm*, 68; *ḍalâlah*, 65; *ḍalla*, 65; *ḍallala*, 66; *ḍâllîn*, 66; *iḍlâl*, 66

David (Prophet Dâwûd)
  condemning the violation of God's commandments, 52
  praising God, 14

Day of Judgment
  benefits of remembering, 17, 18

Day of Judgment (*continued*)
God's sovereignty over, 17, 47
none can benefit nor harm another on, 46–47
various Quranic contexts of, 50

Day of Resurrection, 16

Dhû'l-Qarnayn, 54

Dîn (دين)
defined, 49
linguistic derivatives of, in Quran: *al-dîn*, 47, 50; *al-dîn al-khâlis*, 50; *al-dîn al-qayyim*, 50; *dayn*, 50; *dîn*, 49–50; *dîn al-ḥaqq*, 50; *dîn Allâh*, 50; *tadâyantum*, 51; *Yawm al-Dîn*, 47, 50;

Disbelief, 26, 42
neglect of praising God, 42
pattern of, 26

Disbelievers, 35, 48, 52, 54, 66, 68
alleging Quran was forged, 54
among Children of Israel, 52
among People of the Book, 52
assigning female names to angels, 35
doubting the resurrection, 66
God's wrath upon, 64
of Quraysh, 48, 54
regret in the Hereafter, 68

English language
idiom of, 1
translations of the Quran, *xvi–xviii*

Eve. *See* Adam (and Eve)

Fasting (*Ṣiyâm*), 22

Al-Fâtiḥa
affirmation of divine covenant, 11
Arabic text of, 29
central prayer of, 23, 61
chronology of revelation, 8–9
God's answer to the human cry, 18
greatest chapter of the Quran, 10, 31
guide to the universe of the Quran, 11
guiding the Prophet and believers, 9
in healing the sick, 31
impact on believers, 11
impact on the Prophet, 9
moral center of the Quran, 12
moral obligation of, 20
Mother of the Book, 31
names of, 10–11
one of two lights of revelation, 9
personal prayer, 7
in Prayer (*Ṣalât*), 10, 28, 29–30
in praying for rain, 31–32
principal words of, 34
promise to uphold truth, 12
Quranic style of, 9
summary of the Quran, *xviii*
teaches how to be grateful, 11
theme(s) of, 1, 11, 23, 28, 33
vocabulary of worship, 33
warning to humanity, 8

Fetus, developing for an established term, 36

God. *See* Allah (God)

Gospel of Jesus, 9, 60

Gratitude
to Allah, 14, 63
bringing harmony, 15
to creation, 14–15
for life's treasures, 14
model of, 15

Ḥadîth of the Prophet ﷺ. (*See* "Ḥadîth Index")

Ḥajj. *See* Pilgrimage (*Ḥajj*)

Ḥamd (حمد)
defined, 41
linguistic derivatives of, in Quran: *Aḥmad*, 42; *ḥamd*, 42;

Ḥamd (حمد) (*continued*)
Maqâm Maḥmûd, 42; *Muḥammad*, 41
See also Praise
Hammad, Ahmad Zaki, *xvii*
Ḥanafî ruling on saying *Âmîn* after al-Fâtiḥa, 30
Hebrew, 37
Hell
disbelievers cast into, 68
overpass above, 58
path of those who reject guidance, 55
Hereafter. *See* Afterlife (Hereafter)
Ḥirâ', Cave of, 8
Hypocrites
likened to those in a storm, 60
prohibition of standing over the graves of, 59
standing lazily in prayer, 60
Ibn ʿAbbâs, on praise, 14
Ibn Kathîr, on guidance, 23
Ibn Masʿûd, 30
Ibn Muʿalla. *See* Abû Saʿîd Ibn Muʿalla
Ibn Nawfal. *See* Waraqa Ibn Nawfal
Ibrâhîm. *See* Abraham
Idolatry, as clear misguidance, 66
Idols
deception, 68
exposed by Joseph as false deities, 35
fruitless worship of, 52
worshipped by Abraham's father, 26
Ihdinâ (إهدنا)
definition of, 55
linguistic derivatives of, in Quran: *hadîyya*, 56; *hady*, 56; *hudâ*, 55–56; *ihdinâ*, 34, 55
Interpretation, definition of, 1
Isaac and Ishmael (Prophets Isḥâq and Ismâʿîl)
and Abraham, 14
model of grace, 25
Ishmael (Prophet Ismâʿîl). *See* Isaac and Ishmael
Islam
distinctive dimension of, 9
revealed religion, 50, 55
as the straight way, 61
sweep of, 33
Ism (اسم)
defined, 35
linguistic derivatives of, in Quran: *asmâ'*, 35, 38; *bismillâh*, 34–36, 38; *ism*, 34–36; *musammâ*, 36; *samâ'*, 35; *samîyya*, 35; *samma*, 35
Jacob (Prophet Yaʿqûb)
accused of delusions, 68
model of grace, 25
relying on God, 54
Jesus (Prophet ʿÎsâ)
calling his people to worship Allah, 58
condemning the violation of God's commandments, 52
as a mercy, 40
model of grace, 25
teachings forsaken, 26
John (Prophet Yaḥyâ)
model of grace, 25
Jonah (Prophet Yûnus), 65
Joseph (Prophet Yûsuf)
allegedly eaten by a wolf, 54
entrusted with authority, 46
exposing idols, 35
forsaking the ways of disbelievers, 61
questioning prisonmates, 44

Khadijah, wife of the Prophet, 9
Al-Khudry. *See* Abû Saʿîd al-Khudry
Lâ ilâha illa'Allah
  real meaning of, *xv, xviii*
Linguistic precedence, 37
Loan arrangements, recording of, 51
Lord. *See* Allah (God), lordship of; *Rabb* (رَبّ)
Madinah, 9, 26, 62
Maghdûb (مَغْضُوب)
  defined, 64
  linguistic derivatives of, in Quran: *ghadab,* 64–65; *maghdûb,* 64–65
Makkah, 5, 8
Al-Makkî, Mujâhid, 9
Mâlik (مَالِك)
  defined, 45
  linguistic derivatives of, in Quran: *mâ malakat aymânuhum,* 47; *malaka,* 45; *malik,* 47; *Mâlik al-Mulk,* 46; *Mâlik Yawm al-Dîn,* 47, 50; *malk,* 45; *milk,* 45; *mulk,* 45–46; *mulkan kabîra,* 47
Mâlikî ruling on saying *Âmîn* after al-Fâtiḥa, 30
Maqâm Maḥmûd. See Station of Praise
Mary (Maryam)
  model of grace, 25
  named by her mother, 35
Mercy
  bestowed on creation, 16
  See also Allah (God), mercy of
Methodology of Islamic Art, xiv
Methodology of Islamic Education, xiv
Models of grace, 25
Moral contract, 17–20, 24
Moses (Prophet Mûsâ)
  instructing his people to seek God's help, 54
  laws abandoned, 26
  model of grace, 25
  outraged with the Israelites worshipping golden calf, 65
  the Quranic story of the mountain, *xi–xii*
Motherhood, nature of, 39
Mount of Light, 8
Muḥammad, linguistic meaning of, 42
Muḥammad ﷺ (Prophet). *See* Prophet Muḥammad ﷺ (Messenger of Allah)
Muḥammad Quṭb, *xi*
Muslims. *See* Believers and Muslims
Mustaqîm (مُسْتَقِيم)
  defined, 58
  linguistic derivatives of, in Quran: *qâ'im,* 58; *qâma,* 58, 60; *qawm,* 61; *qiyâm,* 58, 60; *al-Qayyûm,* 61; *al-Ṣirâṭ al-Mustaqîm,* 58–59, 61
Naʿbud (نَعْبُد)
  defined, 51
  linguistic derivatives of, in Quran: *ʿabd,* 51; *ʿibâda,* 51; *ʿIbâdatullâh,* 52; *naʿbud,* 51
Nastaʿîn (نَسْتَعِين)
  defined, 53
  linguistic derivatives of, in Quran: *aʿâna,* 53; *ʿawân,* 53; *ʿawn,* 53–54; *istiʿâna,* 54; *ʿuwn,* 53
Niʿma (نِعْمَة)
  defined, 62
  linguistic derivatives of, in

Quran: *naʿîm*, 63; *niʿam*, 62; *niʿma*, 62–63

Noah (Prophet Nûḥ)
- Ark of, 38
- model of grace, 25
- praising God, 14
- rejected by his people, 67

Non-Muslims
- right to accurate depiction of Islam, *xviii*

On the Islamic Interpretation of History, *xiv*

Overview, definition of, 1

People of the Book
- splintered into sects, 52
- stand upon nothing, 60
- *See also* Children of Israel; Christians

People of grace, characteristics of, 25–26, 67

People of wrath, characteristics of, 26, 67

Pharaoh
- misleading people, 68
- Moses describing God to, 68
- passing death sentence, 54

Pilgrimage (*Ḥajj*)
- glorifying the name of Allah during, 38
- rite of worship, 22

Praise
- neglect of, 52
- volitional and conscious, 42
- warning against seeking unmerited praise, 42
- *See also* *Ḥamd* (حمد); Allah (God), praise of

Prayer (*Ṣalât*)
- definition of, 10
- and al-Fâtiḥa, 10, 29
- founded on devotion to God, 59
- hypocrites in, 60

Pre-Islamic era, 48
- as Days of Ignorance, 48
- usage of the name *Allah*, 37

Prophet Muḥammad ﷺ (Messenger of Allah)
- bestowed name of *Aḥmad*, 42
- confiding in Khadijah, 9
- exhorting his companions to seek God's help, 22
- Farewell Address of, 27
- first encounter with Angel of Revelation 8
- given voice in al-Fâtiḥa, 9
- instructed to ordain worship, 52
- mercy to the worlds, 40
- model of gratitude, 15
- model worshipper, 22
- parable of the straight way, 23
- saying *Âmîn* in Prayer, 30
- seeking God's help against the Quraysh, 54
- and the Station of Praise, 42–43
- trust left to every Muslim, 27

Prophets
- Aaron (Hârûn), 25
- Abraham (Ibrâhîm), 14, 25–27, 35, 60, 67
- alerting against misguidance, 67
- David (Dâwûd), 14, 52
- exemplifying the way of Allah, 67
- Isaac (Isḥâq), 14, 25
- Ishmael (Ismâʿîl), 14, 25
- Jacob (Yaʿqûb), 25, 54, 68
- Jesus (ʿÎsâ), 25–26, 40, 52, 58
- John (Yaḥyâ), 25
- Joseph (Yûsuf), 35, 44, 46, 54, 61
- Moses (Mûsâ), *xi–xii*, 25–26, 40, 54, 56, 65, 68
- Noah (Nûḥ), 14, 25, 38, 67
- path of, 57
- pleasing to God, *xii*
- purity of, *xii*

Prophets (*continued*)
Shuʿayb, 57
Solomon (Sulaymân), 14, 46
Zechariah (Zakarîya), 25
See also individual entries of the Prophets by name

Psalms, 9

Queen of Sheba, 47

Quran
detailing inheritance rules, 68
final revelation, 7, 64
first words revealed of, 12
inimitable style of, *xii, xv*
as a mercy, 40
mutually illuminating, 2
reminder for those who resolve to be straight, 59
student of, 33
system of life in, *xiv*
transcending barriers, 24
translations of, *xv–xvi*
universality of, 33
verses revealed before al-Fâtiḥa, 8

Quranic commandments, 58

Quraysh
besieging Muslims in Madinah, 62
defeated by Muslims at Badr, 48
falsely ascribing to Allah and His Messenger, 54

Rabb (رَبّ)
definition of, 43
as a frequent reference for God, 43
linguistic derivatives of, in Quran: *arbâb*, 44; *rabâ'ib*, 43; *rabb*, 43–45; *rabbânî*, 44; *rabîb*, 43; *ribbi*, 44; *ribbiyyûn*, 44

Al-Raḥîm (الرّحيم). *See Al-Raḥmân*

Al-Raḥmân (الرّحمن), *al-Raḥîm* (الرّحيم),
defined, 39–41
linguistic derivatives of, in Quran: *arḥâm*, 39; *dhû al-raḥma*, 39; *marḥama*, 39; *raḥim*, 39; *râḥim*, 39; *raḥma*, 39; *raḥmân*, 39
most often cited attribute of Allah, 40

Revealed truth
manipulation of, 26

Revelation
Angel of, 8
final one, 7, 64
greatest blessing conferred to humanity, 64
highest knowledge, 64

Rules (*aḥkâm*) related to al-Fâtiḥa, 29–30

Ṣalât. *See* Prayer (*Ṣalât*)

Salsabîl, 35

Satan
Abraham's warning not to worship Satan, 27
enemy of humanity, 68
leading people astray, 68
obstacle on the straight way, 61
prime seducer of people, 68
true believers safe from, 53

Shuʿayb, Prophet, 57

Ṣirât (صراط)
defined, 57
linguistic derivatives of, in Quran: *Ṣirât*, 57–58; *Ṣirâṭ'l-Jaḥîm*, 57; *Ṣirâṭî*, 57; *Ṣirâṭi-Rabbik*, 57; *Ṣirâṭillâh*, 57

Ṣiyâm. *See* Fasting (*Ṣiyâm*)

Solomon (Prophet Sulaymân)
praising God, 14
praying for an earthly kingdom, 46

Station of Praise, 42–43
The straight way
  adherents of, 24
  commandment to adhere to, 58
  defined, 61
  moral objective of, 25
  parable of, 23
  path of all the prophets, 57
  Satan an obstacle on, 61
  waymarks of, 7
Studies in Human Psychology, xiv
Al-Ṭabarî, on praising God, 13
Tafsîr. *See* Commentary literature
Thankfulness. *See* Gratitude
Torah, of Moses, 40
Universe, worshipping, 11, 15
Vocabulary Reference, definition of, 2
Waraqa ibn Nawfal, 9
Womb
  developing fetus within, 36
  linguistic origin of *raḥim*, 39
  sustaining life before birth, 39
Worship
  and Almsgiving (*Zakât*), 22, 61
  assumes commitment, 22
  conserving relations, 21
  and Fasting (*Ṣiyâm*), 22
  moderation in, 21
  and Pilgrimage (*Ḥajj*), 22, 38, 56–57
  and Prayer (*Ṣalât*), 10, 22, 28–29, 54, 59, 61
  preserving purity, vision, and equilibrium, 21
  principal objective of life, 52
  protection from evil, 53
  relationship to love, 51–52
  rites of, 22
  sanctuary of human existence, 19
  saving the human being from ruin, 21
  scope of, 20
  strength of when reflecting on God's greatness, 52
  timelessness of, 20
  vocabulary of, 33
  wellspring of good behavior, 52
Worshipper(s)
  asking Allah not to cause their hearts to swerve, 56
  dialogue with Allah, 7
  in need of Allah, 23
  on the path of righteousness, 27
  reaching peak of human goodness, 24
Wrath
  Quranic contexts regarding Allah's wrath, 64
  in reference to the Children of Israel, 26, 67
  See also Allah, wrath of; *Maghḍûb*; People of wrath
Yawm (يوم)
  defined, 48
  eschatological usages, 48
  linguistic derivatives of, in Quran: *ayyâm*, 48; *yawm*, 47–48
  temporal signification of, 49
Zakât. *See* Almsgiving (*Zakât*)
al-Zamakhsharî,
  on chronology of al-Fâtiḥa's revelation, 9
  on guidance, 22–23

ACKNOWLEDGMENTS

My Lord, dispose me to give thanks for Your grace, with which You have graced me and my parents, and that I do righteous deeds with which You are pleased. And enter me, by Your mercy, among Your righteous servants.

— The Quran, 27:19

This book was written as a pilot to the work *The Quran: Interpretation in Context,*™ a completely new interpretation of the Quran in English. The aim is simply to provide English-speaking readers from all walks of life and in every season with access to the crystalline message of the Quran in the most vigorous language of our era. This is the first fruit of what has become known to many as The Quran Project,™ itself a premier endeavor of the Quranic Literacy Institute (QLI).™ Over the years, the many sincere and serious men and women, young and old, who have become part of the growing family of the Quranic Literacy Institute have nurtured a special love for the Gracious Quran and a deep reverence for its message and its Messenger ﷺ. I therefore find myself indebted to more people than I can possibly name here regarding the preparation of this book. In particular, I am beholden to both Ibrahim Abusharif and Amer Haleem, whose editorial assistance, professional integrity, and devoted companionship have been a blessing in life and whose continued company I hope for in the highest stations of the Garden. My research assistant, Jamal Sawaf, has given me many reasons to be thankful to him and to his family. The volunteer energies of Siamak Kargar are also a cause for gratitude. I am grateful, as well, to Noah Keller for his reading of the earliest version of this manuscript and suggesting valuable adjustments that enabled me to make important revisions and confirmed me in the vision of this and the larger work. A vote of gratitude goes to Zeba Siddiqui as well for her insightful reading and comments on a fairly developed manuscript. Abd al-Hakim Jackson deserves special mention for his early help in bringing to my attention insights regarding the Vocabulary Reference and for his reading of a near-final manuscript. Also, A. R. Kidwai's keen review of the manuscript was valuable and informed. Also, I extend much thanks to Gaylord Toft who read the entire manuscript at various stages and provided me with valuable observations. Likewise, Hatem and Bridget El-Gabri were generous in providing me with important insights on an early draft; Hatem, in particular, was a constant source of inspiriting and advice. I was touched by the spirit and special encouragement of Khuram Murad. Willis Gertner's comments and observations of an early manuscript from a comparative-religions aspect were enheartening. I offer thanks as well to Muzzammil Siddiqi who read the manuscript as it was taking final shape and whose remarks on the special merits of a Quranic commentary that evokes "prayerfulness" were especially encouraging. Brief thanks scarcely do justice to the larger effort of Linda Thayer, who closely read the final draft and made many insightful suggestions and thoughtful remarks. Mona Mobarek of Australia read with enthusiasm an early draft, for which I am grateful, as did Mohammad Saleem Kayani, who offered useful opinions. I would like to extend thanks to Betsy Blumenthal for her meticulous service as a proofreader, as well as to Kathryn Kraynic and Tamara Agha-Jaffar. Ann Hutchinson also proofread two different drafts with appreciated diligence. I would like also to express appreciation to Abu Ishaq Abdul Hafiz, Ahmad Eldeib, Alice Sawaf, Aminah Assami, Aminah Jandali, Anas Osman, Balkozar Adam, Elizabeth Martin, Hussein Mansy, Husyn Abiba, Imad Tarabishy, Jackleen Salem, Jamal Badawi, Julia Martin, Khadija Abdul-Rahman, Maneh al-Johani, Mohamad Yusseef, Mohammad A. Cheema, Mohammad Kishta, Mubarak Amine, Muhamad Krad, Muhammad Jaghlit, Nadia Salem, Nahid Khan, Naveed K. Mallick, Osama Hammad, Osama Osman, Pamela Taylor, Robert Crane, Roger Othman, Salma Helm, Samir Hasan, Sarah Shariff, Seema Ahmad, Seema Imam, Tasneema Ghazi, Waheed Fakhri, Yusuf T. DeLorenzo, and Zahra Khudera—all of whom volunteered to read the manuscript and made valuable remarks. Lastly, I reserve sincere and loving appreciation for the skilled proofreading of Salma Hammad, my daughter, who read the manuscript a number of times with a keenness and proficiency that proved invaluable, and Osama Hammad, my son, who applied his creative diligence and awareness of graphic arts to construct the floral pattern used on the outside and inside covers at a critical time before going to press.

QURANIC LITERACY INSTITUTE

The Opening to the Quran commences a series of publications of THE QURAN: INTERPRETATION IN CONTEXT,™ an endeavor of THE QURAN PROJECT™ and a premier undertaking of the QURANIC LITERACY INSTITUTE (QLI).™ QLI's mission—symbolized by its motto "Advancing Islamic Literacy"™—is to alleviate Islamic illiteracy among English-speaking Muslims and other faith communities and, in the words of the QLI Charter, ***"to aid men, women, and families of all creeds and all walks of life to understand the seminal sources of Islam and to help Muslims live Islam as a way of life."***

ALSO BY THE AUTHOR

LASTING PRAYERS
of the Quran and the Prophet Muḥammad ﷺ

The most comprehensive volume of supplications from the Quran and the Prophet Muḥammad ﷺ in the English language, *Lasting Prayers* presents a lucid, bold, and moving account of the Quran's "heroes of prayer" and compiles the supplications of the Prophet ﷺ that cover the full sweep of life's occasions. As reviewer Dr. Linda Thayer wrote:

> *Lasting Prayers* discloses the height and depth, the length and breadth of Islamic spiritual energy. The all-inclusive introduction summons the hesitant to come close to God, to come boldly before his Lord, who stands ever ready to give and to forgive generously. By allowing oneself to become absorbed into the prayers recorded in the Quran and those spoken from the lips of the Prophet Muḥammad ﷺ himself the seeker establishes a dynamic relationship with the Creator. . . . In summary, the compilation of prayers in this comprehensive book serves to teach the 'muslim' to be ever sensitive to his intended purpose on earth, to his own standing before God, to his social interaction, and to the entire creation's incessant need for and welcome access to Allah. One learns how to ask God's blessing for this life and for the Next.

ISLAMIC LAW
Understanding Juristic Differences

While interest in Islamic law is on the rise in the English-speaking world, there remains the need for greater accessibility and understanding of its issues and sources. Of all its aspects, however, least has been written on the topic of *al-Khilâf al-Fiqhi*, the science exploring the world of juristic differences. In *Islamic Law: Understanding Juristic Differences*, Dr. Ahmad Zaki Hammad introduces the major principles governing juristic variance among established schools of law and well-known Muslim jurists, and their different methods of interpreting Texts from the Quran and the statements and deeds of the Prophet Muḥammad ﷺ. *Islamic Law* outlines the major categories of *khilâf*. It then surveys more than a dozen subcategories, delving into actual readings and interpretations of legal Texts from the Quran and statements of the Prophet ﷺ, from the point of view of several schools of Islamic jurisprudence. As Dr. Abd al-Hakim S. Jackson wrote in the preface to the work:

> *Islamic Law* makes a stunning contribution by laying bare the issue of juristic variance, explaining its causes and distinguishing those forms that are legitimate from those that are not. Dr. Hammad guides the reader to a fascinating rediscovery of the spirit of tolerance and mutual recognition in Islam.